T0356292

"Dr. Z has done it again! *The Missing Conversations* is required reading in our organization, and we provide copies to all our business owner clients and their key executives. Maximizing your company's value isn't just about your P&L, it's also about your people and creating an environment of joyful success."

**– NEAL ALBRITTON, CEO, lead advisor, &
joy-bringer at Albritton Financial Services**

"*The Missing Conversations* is more than a book, it's a guide for leaders navigating modern complexities. Powerful storytelling and brief, action-oriented chapters offer reflection questions and actionable takeaways that were crafted for leaders on the go. It's a game changer for anyone ready to tackle essential conversations shaping personal and organizational growth."

**– DAVID PONDER, partner and cofounder of
Cential Consulting**

"*The Missing Conversations* will help those in your leadership team improve the way they communicate, allowing them to work smarter to achieve goals. Dr. Z's real-life stories and examples make the book a must read for business leaders."

**– STEVE YOUNG, president and owner of
Deca Realty**

"In *The Missing Conversations*, Dr. Z dives deep into the unseen dynamics that shape the success or failure of teams and organizations. He brings a rare mix of insight and practicality, revealing how open dialogue can empower teams, drive innovation, and build sustainable success. Several of these conversations have even become pillars by which I manage my standing monthly team meetings!"

– ADRIAN GLASS, founder and CEO of The Post Sportsbar & Grill

"George Bernard Shaw's insight, "The single biggest problem in communication is the illusion that it has taken place," highlights a common pitfall where we assume our messages are understood, yet others leave with different interpretations, causing misunderstandings and costly errors. *The Missing Conversations* is essential for business leaders who want to ensure their teams achieve true understanding through effective dialogue. This book is a vital tool for preventing the cascading issues that arise from poor communication."

– BILL REICHMUTH, director of global physical security at Reinsurance Group of America

"After thirty years as a communication expert, I still find myself experiencing "guppy moments," when my mouth opens but nothing comes out. *The Missing Conversations* offers leaders specific communication strategies to turn these moments into productive conversations."

– DR. PAAIGE TURNER, provost and executive vice president for academic affairs at Aurora University

"Many high-performing leaders get frustrated as they scale their businesses, focusing on the challenges ahead while the opportunity cost of unspoken conversations grows rapidly. In this book, Zach highlights these often overlooked (or ineffectively executed) conversations and provides leaders with an easily digestible, thought-provoking, and actionable approach to unleash their people and accelerate the business. The questions posed in the book will ignite the leader's passion and, when shared with the team, foster increased alignment around the essential conversations we're often missing. Use this book as a tool to increase leverage, decrease friction, and drive your results on purpose."

– JOHN REGAN, vice president of people development and strategic planning at Keeley Companies

THE
MISSING
CONVERSATIONS

THE
MISSING
CONVERSATIONS

Navigating Awareness, Avoidance,
and Adversity at Work

ZACHARY A. SCHAEFER, PhD

Published by Worth Books, an imprint of Forefront Books, Nashville, Tennessee.

Distributed by Simon & Schuster.

Library of Congress Control Number:2024924543

Print ISBN: 978-1-63763-195-9
E-book ISBN: 978-1-63763-196-6

Cover Design by George Stevens, G Sharp Design LLC
Interior Design by Bill Kersey, KerseyGraphics

Printed in the United States of America

DEDICATION

To Kizzy, for inspiring and reminding me to practice what I preach in our home, as well as in the workplace, through your patient communication, abundant understanding, and natural acceptance.

Contents

SECTION 3: ADVERSITY

SECTION 4: PART OF A SYSTEM

INTRODUCTION

"WE'VE GOT TO GROW OUR WAY OUT OF THIS HOLE," the confident CEO exclaimed. The rest of the leadership team nodded silently in agreement. She stood up from her seat and walked over to the whiteboard covered in printouts of financial models, with arrows and trend lines pointing in the wrong direction.

"Our strategy is grow, grow, grow. Not growing is *not* acceptable. No, it is worse than that. It is surrender, it is death to our company," she continued. "Hit the goals! Make the numbers! We are all in this together!" Her energy was rising to a crescendo, and the leaders around the finely grained oak table in the middle of the boardroom seemed to be feeding off that energy. They were exhibiting the common nonverbal behaviors that signal emotional alignment, such as a flurry of head nods, smiles, eye contact, and forward posturing.

"So, what is our strategy?" she asked her team, hoping the enthusiastic nonverbals she was witnessing would translate into an equally enthusiastic response.

Six sets of eyes instantly broke eye contact and looked down to inspect the table, clearly believing inspiration and answers were hidden in the wood grain. The only sound in the room now was paper shuffling. After a full five-seconds of silence (that felt more like ten minutes), the CFO and HR Director both said, "Grow or die." They meant it as a statement, but everyone could practically *hear* the question mark at the end, as the pitch of their voices took an unexpected turn upward.

Overlooking the implied question hanging in the air—which everyone else understood to mean they were less in agreement with her strategy and more questioning whether it *was* a strategy—the CEO jumped in, "Yes, that is what I'm talking about!"

The next twenty-five minutes were spent discussing the tactical actions to hit their current goals and stop revenue levels from dropping. The mimicry of the CEO's energy faded as quickly as it had emerged once the team started burrowing into the details of hitting quarterly sales quotas and putting out the operational fires of the day.

Being in the consulting and coaching business over the last twenty years, I have been fortunate enough to listen to and learn from thousands of conversations like the one above. I have seen the good, the bad, and the ugly of leadership-team communication practices, the conversations that form the decision-making vehicles that drive companies either to success…or off a cliff.

Many leaders do not realize they are in the business of *consistent, effective decision-making* and put very little analysis into their team's communication norms—what they talk about, how they talk about it, and what they aren't talking about. This type of leadership communication apathy is common, and it has a direct impact on their company's financial statements and culture. Luckily, though, it is easily fixable. Better yet, it is *preventable* with a few simple steps that you will learn throughout this book.

I have served in a variety of unique business roles that have positioned me to observe and participate in leadership communication from a variety of perspectives, including high-stakes meeting facilitator, conflict mediator, leadership behavior coach, project-based management consultant, soft skills trainer. Each of these roles allows me to establish deep trust with clients that gives me the ability to uncover how their leadership communication enables or constrains their decision-making and goal execution.

Being a trusted advisor to these leaders has given me a window into their private thoughts. Many times, I've found the leaders I'm working with are thinking the complete opposite of what their peers are thinking, even when they are on the same leadership team! The worst part is that they all *believe* they are aligned.

Through these intimate conversations and consulting engagements, I've learned that organizations fail to execute on their goals less because of what they *are* talking about and more because of what they *aren't* talking about—and because of what they are assuming.

The most important conversations we should be having in the workplace are usually the ones that are missing. We will dig into the three reasons they are missing—one of which is much more problematic and difficult to change than the other two—and provide you with simple decision-making and conversational tools along the way to help you start growing better conversations at your company.

I know that missing conversations can revitalize a business because that's what I do for a living, and I have participated in the evidence-based stories presented in this book. I know it can help your business clarify focus, create leadership alignment, and recalibrate your accountability standards to judge your company's success, because when done well, these conversations spark success. When neglected or conducted hastily, they lead to decay, atrophy, and incremental decline.

Personal and organizational growth is contingent on the type and quality of conversations we are having. We get out of conversations what we put into them.

Figure 1. Grow the essential conversations, prune the rest.

Conversations are organic, dynamic, and alive. When engaged with energy and focus, they take on a life of their own and can create deep roots between the people engaged in the discussion. I think about high-quality conversations as **giant timber bamboo**. Even though giant timber bamboo is actually a type of grass, it resembles a skinny tree that appears to grow very slowly and then very fast. But that perception is mistaken because the growth *is* occurring; it is just occurring underground and out of sight. It takes up to three years to establish its underground root system, but once established, the shoots pierce through the surface and can grow up to twelve inches a day until it reaches its maximum height of more than sixty feet in sixty days.[1]

Bamboo is an aggressive subterranean spreader and prolific grower. So, when left untended and neglected, this plant becomes extremely invasive once it establishes its root system. Despite its invasiveness, however, people have figured out how to contain bamboo by laying out underground boundaries and barriers. Humans have learned to harness the invasiveness and turn a negative into a benefit, using bamboo for shade, privacy, and even construction materials.

Harnessing bamboo through barriers and structures that flex the plant into specific forms is similar to how decision trees work. In business settings, decision trees are a tool used to cultivate the right results and effective outcomes because each decision is a branch on a larger decision tree, with certain decisions leading you down a certain branch. Decision trees put ideas, solutions, and opportunities in context by showing a variety of contingencies. They visualize "if *this*, then *that*" logic and help to contextualize

Figure 2. Cultivate the wild growth into a useful design.

potential decisions. By becoming aware of what conversations are missing (that need to be added), you are making a strategic decision to curate your bamboo forest and create conscious growth in a direction you choose. Curating conversations, even if it slows things down at first (it does), is a methodical approach to growth that pays off later, once the conversational fruit starts to visibly grow.

PREVIEW OF BOOK STRUCTURE

I wrote this book specifically for organizational leaders with full schedules. As such, I broke it into bite-size pieces, allowing leaders with packed calendars and shifting priorities to quickly get the gist of individual topics. The chapters are super short, and each one ends with a summary of the missing conversation, as well as a few *Root Questions* that help you immediately apply that chapter's key point to your specific situation.

You'll see several case-study-style examples and anecdotes throughout the book, so I'd like to share a quick word on anonymity, disclosure, and privacy. My career as a consultant and leadership coach is dependent on establishing and maintaining trust, and since I like my job and want to keep doing it in the future, I used a *Frankenstein* approach, bringing together elements from different cases and cutting key pieces of information from single cases, all to protect identities. There are a few times when I'll share more precise information that could possibly be tied to a real person or business. In those instances, I received permission from those clients to share those details, and they have reviewed and signed off on those chapters.

Figure 3. Well-groomed decision trees are great in theory but rarely practiced.

The book is broken up into four sections. The first three focus on the biggest blind spots I've found are responsible for most of the missing conversations in the organizations I've worked with. Those three areas are:

1. Awareness (or lack thereof)
2. Avoidance
3. Adversity

I'll dig into each one in detail and help you identify them in your organization.

In the fourth and final section of the book, I will explain how conversations are part of a larger organizational system. The whole reason humans work together is that we achieve more, faster, when we work together on large goals, when we specialize our knowledge and skills, and when we are willing to both defend and modify our ideas based on situational circumstances.

But that's only possible when our leaders and leadership teams are communicating effectively—among themselves and with the employees in the trenches.

In most organizational settings, leadership *teams* are implied, but they are out of sight. It is sexier to celebrate a single person—often the founder and/or CEO—because this narrative is easier for our brains to grasp. This is because of the structure of the media business, neuroscience, and psychology. Our media environment mirrors our craving for stories, and it is much easier (and more lucrative) to tell the story of a lone hero who embarks on an epic quest to vanquish his or her enemy, thereby saving the masses from untold horrors.

In other words, we as a culture are really into hero worship.

And yet, our species would not be where we are today without team cooperation, structured and civil (i.e., nonviolent) disagreement, and our inherent drive to work with others to achieve big goals. Neuroscientific research has shown that the human brain is wired for social interaction and cooperation. Mirror neurons, for example, play a crucial role in our ability to understand and empathize with others, facilitating teamwork and collaboration.[2] Despite this, when retroactively making sense of our success, we often forsake the messiness of working on a great team and instead focus on a single individual. This is partly due to the brain's tendency to simplify complex social dynamics by attributing success to a clear and identifiable figure, known as the *Fundamental Attribution Error.*[3]

If you don't believe me, just think of all the famous business books and case studies about visionaries, disruptors, geniuses, and gurus. Steve Jobs. Sheryl Sandberg. Elon Musk. Jack Welch. Phil Knight. Frances Hesselbein. Bob Iger. Of course, we can and should learn important lessons from the excellent perspectives shared by these leaders and their biographers, but shouldn't we also hear about the teams around these leaders, the men and women the "hero" relies on to actually make things happen?

How many business books can you name about great leadership *teams*? Thanks to Patrick Lencioni, we know how to identify dysfunctional teams. Thanks to Stephen Covey, we know what individual behaviors to cultivate on our teams. Thanks to Simon Sinek, we know when leaders should eat and what they should start with (our why).

But do we have a single case study detailing how a business *team* worked well together over a long period of time, pushed through challenging communication, broke down organizational politics, set aside egos, and triumphed in the end by adding value, by consistently delighting customers, and by achieving its mission?

Interestingly, there are several books that discuss how music groups who achieved longevity stayed together over the long run. The Grateful Dead. The Allman Brothers. The Beatles. Fleetwood Mac. These books dig into how the individuals came together to make something bigger than any one member while overcoming personal and interpersonal challenges along the way.

While we should all want to see a book about how a purposely built team drives the desired results and creates repetitive value and consistent success, that's a future project. What *this* book will give you and your team is a framework to have higher-quality conversations that directly and positively impact your business.

In short, this book gives you a tool for cultivating a great leadership team.

To do that, though, we've got to get down to the root of the problems that are preventing us from communicating with each other.

So…let's start digging.

SECTION 1:

AWARENESS

*"What gets us into trouble is not what we don't know.
It's what we know for sure that just ain't so."*
—MARK TWAIN

Most leaders are simply not aware that they could be having specific conversations to improve their businesses. This lack of awareness often takes the form of mistaking *urgency* for *strategic action*. Those two things are not the same, and an overreliance on making decisions from a place of urgency will remove strategy from the workplace.

There are two problems layered into this insight: a personal layer and an organizational layer. Without awareness of one's personal leadership strengths and areas for improvement, the leader's personal behavioral growth will eventually become a bottleneck to organizational growth. On the organizational layer, without the right conversations to clarify goals, priorities, and plans, individuals and teams will focus on immediate, urgent tasks rather than on strategic, long-term initiatives. This creates a *reactive* rather than *proactive* approach to decision-making and goal setting. A lack of awareness always leaves you behind the eight ball.

CHAPTER 1

LISTENING OR WAITING TO ATTACK

JAKE IS ONE OF THE NICEST GUYS ON THE PLANET—AND one of the sharpest. He is a quiet fighter, a person who doesn't bring attention to himself when struggling or winning. He just keeps making progress toward his goals, one subtle step at a time. Jake is one of those people who aced standardized tests, has a natural knack for figuring out complex systems, and can persuade and influence others through his expert use of metaphors. He also happens to be my closest friend of more than thirty-four years and a two-time cancer survivor, beating it at seventeen years old and again at nineteen.

Jake is now a successful businessman who co-founded a multimillion-dollar consulting firm, a loving father and husband, and a former terrible listener. His rapid-fire cognitive skills, politeness, general likability, and passion for argumentation served as the perfect cover for his listening deficiency. When he should have been seeking to understand another's point of view, he was organizing his next metaphor to poke holes in a person's ideas or assembling the mental spring needed to jump to his idea, which of course was an improved version of whatever the person talking to him was saying. We all do this to some degree, but Jake had earned his doctorate in using the time when someone else was speaking to hone his rebuttal.

So, when Jake decided to formally engage me as his leadership coach, we had to establish clear boundaries. I also had to warn him that what he learned about himself might not match his version of reality, and that there was no arguing with the cold, hard data we'd collect. To get better, people need to hear the unvarnished truth (at the right time). When we are ready to change, the sugarcoated version that our brains crave is not what leads to behavioral or organizational improvement.

The missing conversation for Jake was not an external one with another person but an internal one revolving around his need to add value, please others, and be viewed as a proactive problem solver. Jake was unaware he was a poor listener. The problem was that the more "proactive" he tried to be, the less he listened to other people's point of view. I knew this as his longtime friend, but anecdotal ingredients don't make for useful behavior-change recipes. So, we collected data from his business partners, employees, and immediate family members.

Because I'm not a therapist and don't ask my coaching clients to lie on a couch, I'm not interested in understanding *why a person is the way they are*; instead, I am interested in *what they are doing* that is problematic (in an organizational setting). With that knowledge, we can work together to develop a plan to help them do things differently. I am a

What and How coach, not a *Why Guy*. The reasons behind our behaviors can have deep roots, and if that is what you need help with or are interested in, be sure to consult a qualified therapist who is skilled at unpacking the root causes of problematic communication behaviors. There is enormous value in exploring why; it's just not my field of expertise and not what my clients are searching for.

As part of my coaching process, I always measure *problematic* communication behaviors and *productive* communication behaviors, and then I sit down and review the data with my client. You can feel the anxiety in the air in those meetings. I am always happy for my clients when a singular pattern is identified, because that is usually the root cause of other problematic communication behaviors that will naturally work themselves out once the negative root is pruned. The big hurdle for them is learning that they've got a problem literally everyone around them sees—but they can't see themselves. Discovering one's lack of awareness is not always a comfortable form of self-evolution.

This was the case with Jake.

The results were clear: 90 percent of the participants we polled ranked "Not Listening" as his most problematic leadership behavior.

Jake disagreed with these findings at first, which is common. He argued that he listens when others share ideas and merely tries to make connections with them. But as we worked through his natural communication style, he quickly realized that *his* listening reality was very different than what others perceived. And perception builds reality.

After digesting the data and realizing he needed (and wanted) to change, we created two goals for Jake. They were to (a) listen with intent and (b) listen to connect. As the saying goes, seek first to understand, then to be understood. Jake had to shift his listening strategy from "waiting to attack" to "listening with purpose." We employed a variety of daily tactics to help Jake pursue this strategy and achieve his goals. He used (and uses) strategic silence, purposeful pauses, a willingness to put his ideas on ice, minimal responses, paraphrase-only, and asking better questions.

These tools enhanced his communication skills and created a clear awareness around the first- and second-order consequences of effective listening. His desired first-order consequence was a deeper mutual respect, trust, and rapport between Jake and his partners, employees, and clients. His second-order consequences included:

- Talent optimization to better match his team talent to project need.
- Deeper understanding of team member capability and capacity.
- Ability to disagree without causing overt (or private) resentments.
- Better resource allocation by not having to address the negative consequences of lost money, time, and human capital through poor project assignments and expectations (that would result from not listening).

We put a plan in place for Jake to work on these things, and he got to work.

The data we collected on Jake's leadership behaviors eighteen months later painted quite a different picture. Every participant unanimously agreed that

Jake had not only improved his listening skills, but that he had become an *excellent* listener, able to seamlessly make connections between current and past conversations. People felt understood, people felt valued. It is no surprise that his consulting firm had more than 50 percent compound annual growth (CAGR) over those same eighteen months.

His lack of listening had festered into multiple areas of his life because of his lack of self-awareness with this skill. To prevent this from recurring, Jake now journals and speaks with a coach every night to take inventory for his day, with a specific focus on listening. While listening still isn't his natural behavior (his words, not mine), he has created mechanisms to overcome that deficiency.

In order to prioritize listening and reap the rewards from it, Jake had to become self-aware and consistently take action on that self-awareness over time. It wasn't a single battle; it was (and is) a war against a behavioral default. We employed Aristotle's *golden mean* principle as a strategy for launching a strong offensive against his problematic listening. In short, to achieve a consistent new behavior that does not come naturally to someone and to eliminate a negative behavior (vice), we must first shoot far beyond what is necessary and strive for unnatural behaviors on the opposite end of the spectrum (virtue). Then, after we've built some behavioral muscle, we can shift our sights back to the middle, or what Aristotle called the *golden mean*. This process takes time and only works with commitment and consistency, but Jake was steadfast in addressing the behavior he wanted to change. Once we shifted to his "manageable middle" listening goals, he was already enjoying the benefits of better listening and had no intention of ever going back to his old pattern of *waiting-to-attack* listening.

Root Questions

- From your perspective, what are your most *productive* leadership communication behaviors?
- From your perspective, what are your most *problematic* leadership communication behaviors?
- Where did your answers to the above questions come from? (e.g., your intuition, your perception of reality, patterns that emerged from systematic data collection)
- If someone could help you identify problematic behaviors that are stifling workplace relationships and results, would you want that knowledge?

Missing Conversation Quick Facts

CATEGORY	AWARENESS
Missing Conversation	Listening Is a Key Part of Leading and Learning
What It Does	Being an effective listener helps leaders build higher-performing teams and monitor their markets more effectively.
Why It Matters	Leaders who refuse to listen will eventually lose connection with their customers, market share, talented team members, and go out of business.

CHAPTER 2

UNCHAIN THE CHART

Many organizations, especially organizations experiencing rapid growth and scaling, do not spend enough time talking about their organizational structure or organizational chart, also known as an accountability chart.

There are two different features of an accountability chart that are relevant to organizations—and even more important for fast-scaling companies. This tool represents a chain of authority. With a single glance, a well-developed chart can clarify who can make different types of decisions (authority), who has access to the purse strings (budget), and who can work with vendors and sign off on projects. I often refer to this feature of org charts as *signature power*.

While that's important, an equally and sometimes more important feature of an organizational chart is its *chain of communication*, or who should talk to who, about what, and when. Some organizations will have a rigid authority, hierarchy, and structure but a loose communication chain in which a tier-one employee can go to the CEO's office and have a conversation to get something done.

Tesla and SpaceX are examples of companies that have rigid authority structures and flexible communication expectations. They coach and expect their employees to have direct conversations with the people who can solve problems, not to follow a specific chain of command. At the other end of the extreme is the military, which exhibits both a formal and structured chain of command for decision-making and a formal chain of communication for problem-solving. While this slows down problem-solving, it also saves lives. With human life on the line, it doesn't make sense to allow tier-one team members to jump the chain and offer suggestions for change.

Of course, there are specific units within the military that embrace the more open communication chain, but that is the exception to the rule and is only effective with smaller teams consisting of special forces (e.g., Green Berets, SWCC, SEAL, Marine Raiders) who have gone through the most rigorous training to become subject matter experts in strategic and tactical responses, their gear, and their interaction expectations as a team. Going through in-depth training with small groups of people cements trust in a way that makes reliance on organizational tools—like an org chart—unnecessary.

Nonmilitary organizations usually exhibit either the formal authority feature of an org chart or the formal communication expectation from the chart, but rarely both. When that occurs, when there is a lack of awareness around the relationship between chain of command in terms of authority and the chain of communication, organizational politics[4] increases. This produces fertile ground for the game of influence, overshadowing the game of merit and results. Instead of focusing on problem-solving, people focus on taking credit.

Organizational politics is about the art of influence to expand one's power. People achieve this by expanding their authority and control in organizational settings beyond their subject matter expertise or positional authority. And that is much easier to achieve when authority expectations and communication expectations are unclear. People take advantage of these clarity vacuums through likability (popularity), resource hoarding, hollow collaborations, and other forms of covert manipulation.[5]

A common missing conversation that fast-growing organizations overlook involves clearly discussing the dual purpose of their org chart for authority, decision-making, and responsibility, as well as around communication norms and expectations. These last two topics need to be communicated on an ongoing basis.

My client Martin was the vice president of business development at a scaling chemical manufacturer that was adding a new product line into its current market. In years prior, Martin had a lot of authority and discretion to make decisions, but because the company had gone through some strategic growth via acquisitions, the increased headcount led to additional standards and procedures (bureaucracy). A mostly flat organization suddenly had three more layers between executive leadership and tier-one employees, the people combining chemicals in the laboratory.

Martin followed the formal authority hierarchy clearly because it was straightforward and messaged within and across multiple internal communication channels (i.e., internal Slack channels, department meetings, town halls, visibly posted in private areas). But what the company didn't discuss was its communication hierarchy and expectations. Many of the freshly added leaders began to resent Martin because he knew how to get things done, leveraging his institutional knowledge to move projects forward quickly without "taking them up the chain." Interdepartmental animosity emerged, which led to information hoarding, stonewalling, and selective sharing, which of course hurt the company's aggressive business development goals.

As part of our coaching program, I was able to work with Martin and other stakeholders to facilitate conversations between him and the CEO, as well as with the sales team leaders and operations team leaders to help them flesh out their communication guidelines and expectations, especially as that communication flow related to authority expectations and business goals.

These three items—communication flow, authority expectations, and business goals—should never be separated.

These challenging and productive conversations smoothed out a lot of the speed bumps they were experiencing and helped get them back on track to achieving their product rollout. In this case *late* was better than *never*.

Root Questions

- How does your organization use its org chart?
- If you don't have an org chart, what are the reasons behind that decision?
- What can be done to clarify the chain of command/authority in your company?
- How does information flow in your company? How should it flow?
- What is the role of communication in trying to solve cross-functional problems?

Missing Conversation Quick Facts

CATEGORY	AWARENESS
Missing Conversation	Using the Organizational Chart Strategically
What It Does	Helps leadership teams create clarity and accountability throughout their organization.
Why It Matters	Lack of clarity around decision-making authority and allowing a *pass the buck mentality* lead to an organizational death by a thousand cuts.

CHAPTER 3

CALIBRATION CONVERSATIONS (PART 1)

A COMMON THEME THAT KEEPS POPPING UP WITH MY clients revolves around the lack of agreed-upon standards, procedures, and/or rules they can rely on to help govern internal communication and behaviors. Having these type of standards—whether formal and codified or informal and maintained through relationship-based onboarding—should be part of an organization's culture, operations, and value system.

When my coaching clients complain[6] about a coworker or direct report's behaviors, it is often less about the coworker and more about the invisible lowering or elimination of organizational standards that tolerates those type of behaviors. When the majority behaves a certain way most of the time, you're not facing a team member problem; it is a culture problem. And all culture problems are leadership problems.

The lowering or elimination of work performance standards and attitude standards is indicative of leaders who allow suboptimal behaviors to replace standards of excellence. At some point, this environment creates the conditions for poor results, distrust, and celebrating mediocrity as if it is a worthy achievement.[7] These organizational environments are relying on fear and inertia to incentivize workplace behaviors rather than goals and growth.

Bottom line: We get the type of culture we tolerate.

Ben Horowitz's *What You Do Is Who You Are: How to Create Your Business Culture* is my favorite book on organizational culture. It is both philosophically wise and organizationally pragmatic. In it, Ben teaches us that culture is about what we consistently do daily in the workplace. From mundane to milestone decisions, everything is part of culture: communication norms, parking and attire norms, work from home policy, on-site wellness, compensation system, tech stacks (or the lack thereof), how we solve problems, and so on. *Culture* is one of the most misunderstood and oversimplified terms in business for a reason. It is complex and multifaceted. It takes a long time to create and a single decision to ruin.

One of my oldest friends, Jake, whom you met in chapter 1, is also a business partner and my *Life Lab* podcast cohost. We recently recorded a podcast on the topic of excellence, and it dawned on me that while many of my clients have candid conversations around what excellence means for their organization in terms of the results, few of them have similar conversations around what internal communication excellence looks like and, more importantly, what internal communication *sounds* like. This is important, because excellent internal communication—how a company organizes itself—influences and predicts its desired outcomes of excellence.

From a communication perspective, what does excellence sound like when problem-solving, brainstorming, debating, and disagreeing with one another? Dr. Peter Attia wrote a fantastic book called *Outlive*, in which he critiques our society's current approach to medicine and health. He argues our entire medical system is built on a "wait to get sick and then we will treat your symptoms" model that he calls Medicine 2.0, instead of a personalized, preventative approach to creating and maintaining a baseline of health, which he calls Medicine 3.0.[8]

To extend Attia's framework, company leaders often embrace a *Medicine 2.0* approach to communication processes. We don't think about them until they break down. This approach only offers workplace interventions and development opportunities if something goes wrong rather than embracing a *Medicine 3.0* approach. The 3.0 philosophy aims to strengthen and develop systems and relationships *before* they deteriorate, *before* standards grow stale, and *before* a culture of mediocrity emerges.

These are harder conversations to have because most leaders are not aware they should be having them at all. These missing conversations are a result of ignorance rather than omniscience. Fortunately, this is an easy conversational gap to fill and involves stakeholders getting clearer on what excellence looks (and sounds) like for project management communication and effective confrontation communication.[9] These calibration conversations apply to all aspects of your business.

Let me show you what kind of difference simple calibration can make. I love to grill. Imagine I'm grilling up a delicious low-and-slow brisket, and it's crucial that I smoke it for six hours at exactly 275°. I'm counting on my grill thermometer to tell me the correct temperature of the grill. If the thermometer is miscalibrated, I could serve up a nice platter of burnt shoe leather instead of the savory beef dinner my friends and family expect. But if I calibrate the thermometer beforehand to ensure an accurate reading, I'll be the king of the feast and my meat-loving buddies will carry me to the table on their shoulders.

In both grilling scenarios, I'm preparing the meat the same way and cooking it for the same six hours. The only difference is, in the version with the happy ending, I took the time to calibrate my tools before I relied on them.

That's what you need to do with some of the conversations you rely on to move the ball forward at work.

The most straightforward calibration conversation should be performance reviews. But from my experience, these are the most mismanaged conversations in business. When done well, which is rare, these conversations get people back on track to productivity, goal achievement, and skill improvement. It should be a win for the individual and a win for the business. But that is not what usually occurs.

Anxiety, procrastination, outdated and overengineered templates filled out as minimally as possible—this is the norm. And we can't forget the poorly developed structures and anecdotal, one-off observations that tell you more about what the employee did in the past month (recency bias) than how they've performed over the past year.

These conversations:

1. Rarely move the needle on helping someone improve behaviors and skills.
2. Incrementally lower the bar of excellence.
3. Lead to lower productivity and insufficient results.

When executed poorly—which, again, is the norm for performance reviews—the most noticeable results are increased distrust, private resentments, and a bare-minimum mentality.

The sad reality is that most leaders look at performance reviews as an annoying box they have to check off for each employee each year, not as an opportunity to invest in the performance of the men and women on their teams and lead them to greater levels of excellence, efficiency, and reward. They take a compliance-over-commitment approach, only doing performance reviews because they *have* to.[10]

This mindset does not lead to a thriving and productive workplace. Suboptimal performance review processes have been such a common issue for our clients over the last two decades that we developed a performance review diagnostic and design process called *Review Reboot*.

The Review Reboot creates a clear framework for effective performance reviews that is right-sized to a company's capacity and culture. It's a soup-to-nuts approach that starts with conversations around company purpose and strategy, key behaviors and results, how to measure these items, and how to share the data in a way that drives performance and positively impacts culture. That is, our system covers the Why, the What, and the How.

Companies spend too much time engineering KPIs and OKRs (the *what*) and less on how to communicate this information (the *how*) in a way that helps someone get better at their job, enhance their skills, and drive business results. They also completely neglect how this process connects to the company's mission, vision, values, and strategy (the *why*). No one likes to have their behaviors and results critiqued, so it is essential to connect these conversations to the purpose of the business.

Root Questions

- Make a list of the calibration conversations that could be useful to your team. What stands out to you about the list?

- Is the level of formality and structure for your internal processes appropriate for your company's culture?

- Describe how you built your performance review process. (For example, was it built from scratch to fit your culture, or is it a hodgepodge of "best practices" from googled case studies?)

- What do you expect you would learn if you collected anonymous data about your company's current performance review process?

Missing Conversation Quick Facts

CATEGORY	AWARENESS
Missing Conversation	Performance Review Calibration Discussions
What It Does	Gets leadership teams aligned about measuring the things that matter and driving the organization in the right direction.
Why It Matters	Poorly structured performance conversations suck the energy and innovation out of teams. Missing performance conversations are based on a strategy of *hope*; intentional performance conversations lead to the growth of skills and to results.

CHAPTER 4

THIRSTY HORSES

You CAN LEAD A HORSE TO WATER, BUT YOU CAN'T MAKE him drink.

We use this expression to explain a person's inability to fully motivate someone else to action despite providing the necessary tools to get the job done. As usual, conventional wisdom is about half correct.

There are other factors at play behind the scenes of the horse-and-water analogy. First is *how* the horse is being led to the water, or the way the rider is leading him.

Some people have a way with horses; others do not. People with horse sense can anticipate when the horse is actually thirsty, and others learn that through experience. When and how someone brings a horse to water will determine whether it drinks or not. Are we assuming a tight lasso around its neck is an intelligent solution, or are we trying to saddle a wild stallion? Is the rider presenting the horse with fresh water, or is she expecting the horse to drink from a mud puddle? These are all issues around communication and relationship building.

And then there are the many other variables that impact whether that horse will drink or not. Animals have an instinct for when they should eat and drink. If a horse is thirsty, it will drink. If it's not, it won't. The rider can do everything right for all the right reasons, but if the horse isn't interested, then he's just going to stand there.

The classic expression we've all heard a million times isn't really about the horse; it's about the rider. It has more to do with the rider's goals for and perception about what the horse *should* be doing than the horse itself.

It is only through experience that a rider and her horse's perceptions will overlap, and she'll gain some much-needed horse sense from the experience. And since experience is usually all we are left with when we don't get what we want,

You can lead a horse to water, but you can't make him drink.

Figure 4. This wisdom is about communication style and context as well as motivation.

it is safe to assume that an experienced equestrian's understanding of horses comes from the experience of making a lot of mistakes over her career.

If your company has a bunch of thirsty horses, does that suggest your leaders and managers are poor motivators, poor communicators, or have misaligned (or wrong) assumptions about what needs to occur? Does it mean you have the wrong type of horse in the workplace? Are you using a Clydesdale when you need a racehorse?

Is the leader forcing a horse who isn't thirsty to drink from a stream because they don't have the context that the horse just finished eating and drinking?

The ability to motivate someone—be it a horse or a team member—really boils down to that individual's internal motivators, needs, and behaviors, as well as the environmental needs, constraints, and expectations.

To properly motivate on an ongoing basis and ensure people use the tools and resources that an organization provides, you need to understand what makes each person tick. Luckily, there are excellent tools that simplify this process and supplement the longer-term relationship building. My firm is a certified partner with the global workforce assessment company *The Predictive Index*, which has been providing assessments and people analytics since 1955 (one of the oldest assessment companies in the business: accurate and reliable results).

Our talent optimization platform helps you understand a person's drives, needs, and preferred workplace behaviors, as well as how quickly a person learns new information. Through accurate behavioral and cognitive data, it is much easier to work with someone to help them be accountable for their tasks, goals, and mistakes. People analytics help leaders connect, communicate, and motivate their team members.

Leverage is getting more done through others in a way that grows the company and grows the team. To increase your leadership leverage and develop your team members to their potential, you must use valid and reliable people analytics.[11]

If you are banging your head against the wall, thinking you are giving your people everything they need but they are still not doing what you need them to, point the mirror at yourself and think about how you have contributed to the situation (internal conversation) and how well you really know what motivates them.

Human behaviors are flexible, and we shift them situationally without much thought. We alter our behaviors based on our environments even though we'd rather be behaving in different ways. Research shows that the internal drives and needs that form the foundation of our behaviors are much more stable over time,[12] but most people just don't have awareness of that fact. By becoming aware of that information and then taking action on it in the workplace, a lot fewer horses will go thirsty.

Root Questions

- In what ways does your organization think about motivation as a leadership/managerial tool?
- What tools or techniques do you use to understand your team members' natural motivating needs and behaviors?
- Do team members tell you what you want to hear in the moment, make a brief change, and then revert to unproductive or problematic patterns?

Missing Conversation Quick Facts

CATEGORY	AWARENESS
Missing Conversation	How to Do a Task Effectively
What It Does	It allows leaders to focus on how someone is performing an action and the type of relationship and trust they have with a colleague, rather than just trying to motivate someone using general techniques.
Why It Matters	Leaders who understand a person's internal motivating factors and communicate based on those factors have a much greater probability of success building productive workplace relationships that drive results and deepen trust.

CHAPTER 5

NEVER FULFILLED

NOT BEING SATISFIED OR FULFILLED IS OFTEN PART OF the fuel for ambitious people. As long as this feeling is channeled in a productive direction, that internal feeling of restlessness can be used as positive motivation to stay ahead of the competition.

Andy Grove, the co-founder of Intel, talks about this in his book *Only the Paranoid Survive*,[13] and Amy Chua and Jed Rubenfeld highlight the same thing in their book *The Triple Package*.[14] A lack of fulfillment can be useful in a business setting because it keeps a person, team, and company sharp, encourages market-driven innovation based on customer need and desire, and is part of the way you keep your products and services relevant. When unaware of what happens when this mentality is left unchecked, however, this feeling (lack of fulfillment) can be debilitating for companies and the people who run them. This is when the bamboo grows wild and its negative, invasive nature becomes visible.

Like any fuel, unfulfillment can be used positively, like powering the engines that drive our vehicles and machinery, or negatively, such as committing arson. Leaders who lack self-awareness can end up covering themselves in the fuel of unfulfillment and lighting a match, mistakenly thinking they are igniting passion in others when, in reality, they're more likely burning the team to the ground.

Recognizing and celebrating wins, even briefly, is important for company culture and morale. Most people have a point at which they will burn out, the moment their cognitive capacity decreases, and their value to the company switches from accretive to dilutive. From visionaries and builders like Elon Musk to landscapers who maintain company lawns and custodians who sweep the halls, feeling unsatisfied 100 percent of the time wears on a person's soul.

To stay ahead of your competition and retain your company's comparative advantage, it is important to have *some* restlessness from not feeling fulfilled, but it must be accompanied by recognition of small wins and respect for the organizational mission. If not, the unrelenting need to constantly move the goalposts without pausing for a breather leads to self-sabotage and addictive behaviors. An unwavering sense of unfulfillment has its roots in unarticulated values.

As Chua and Rubenfeld discuss in *The Triple Package*, a lack of impulse control is not a good combination when anchored to the pounding drumbeat of *more*. This leads people and teams down dark holes, crippling obsessions, and constant fault finding. We've seen this pattern often, when leaders without integrity encourage their teams to hit their business goals at all costs. Examples include insolvencies such as WorldCom, Tyco, Arthur Andersen, and Enron. Wells Fargo demonstrated the darkest side of unfulfillment-without-integrity when its teams opened millions of fraudulent accounts in order to hit their goals. These situations can be boiled down to poor incentive systems tied to large goals.

These company's leaders were missing conversations about values and principles, including which ones to follow, how team members know when they are following them, and what to do when people get off course. And while goals are like mirages, with new ones emerging farther down the horizon as soon as others are completed, it doesn't mean we can't momentarily embrace a feeling of fulfillment from achieving an immediate goal, even while recognizing there are others to be set.

Root Questions

- What drives your ambition, and how does that impact your sense of fulfillment/satisfaction?
- How do you recognize and celebrate wins in your organization?
- How do you channel your internal drive in a way that promotes innovation and growth while avoiding full-blown burnout?
- What trip wires have you created to pause, reflect, and reassess your goals and strategies before an explosion occurs?

Missing Conversation Quick Facts

CATEGORY	AWARENESS
Missing Conversation	Using Unfulfillment to Highlight Values and Principles
What It Does	Clarifies the operational actions that are necessary, sufficient, and inappropriate for goal achievement.
Why It Matters	Allowing the concept of never being fulfilled to dominate an organization's culture will eventually sanction behaviors adverse to long-term results.

CHAPTER 6

TAXES AND DIVIDENDS

FINANCIAL METAPHORS ARE COMMONPLACE BECAUSE we are all caught in the middle of the web of money. We can't live without it, and it enables and constrains all our choices in daily life, whether we think about it or not. Money itself is an external incentive that causes people to make choices and alter their behaviors to earn more of it.

Money is clearly an incentive system (albeit one the average person doesn't think much about beyond wanting to earn and have more of it), and there are subsystems within money that drive specific actions. Take taxes, the "no-choice fees" we pay to the government. Taxes are a coerced or involuntary incentive system that people pay, despite whether they agree with the tax rate and structure, to stay out of the crosshairs of the law. Everyone is incentivized to pay taxes to stay out of the courtroom and out of prison cells. Few people believe that others can spend our money more appropriately than we can, and yet we give large portions of our income to the government without tracking how the money is spent. Within business, the common ones are income tax, payroll tax, property tax, and excise tax. Business leaders take action and pay these taxes to remain out of trouble with the government, even while most businesses, if they have the financial expertise and deep pockets, do whatever is legally allowable to avoid paying taxes. Tax evasion is not the same as tax avoidance.

Just as we grudgingly pay financial taxes to the government, we are constantly creating subtle *relational taxes* based on our communication habits. When we aren't aware of those around us, when we aren't aware of our attitude and communication style, and when we aren't aware that people have unique needs and ways of getting their work done, we create relational taxes in the workplace.

Carlos was the tax man, and he didn't know it. He was a second-generation American whose parents emigrated from Mexico and arrived in America with a dream and a strong work ethic. They raised him to not take education for granted and to always outwork his peers.

Take initiative, do the task that others won't, and be prepared to work longer and harder. These were the principles ingrained into Carlos from an early age. Fast forward a few decades, and it's no surprise Carlos has built a successful financial services firm that manages more than $1 billion in client assets. He understands how financial taxes work as incentives and as behavior modifiers, because he helps his clients build tax-avoidance strategies every day. Sadly, though, Carlos wasn't paying attention to the relational taxes he was overpaying by not cultivating relationships with his team.

Carlos led his business and his team with a fixed-pie, scarcity mindset. He openly competed with his own employees for the firm's clients, and he routinely took clients away from his employees and added them to his own accounts. This hyper-competitive approach led to high churn at his firm for a decade, which also caused him to take on many lower-level responsibilities that should have been delegated to tier-one employees.

Because everyone knew Carlos would swoop in and take their clients, an atmosphere of minimum effort pervaded the office. This, in turn, led to a process that worked like this:

1. A frustrated employee gave minimal effort.
2. Carlos confronted the team member about their poor performance, but he did so without providing any effective benchmarks or oversight tools to improve.
3. The team member failed to hit Carlos's unspoken performance goals.
4. Carlos personally took over that employee's accounts, causing him further stress and limiting his schedule.

When periodically confronted by his team or industry peers about this pattern, he would fall back on his ethnic heritage, hiding behind his identity by saying, "I'm Mexican, I was born from workers, and I was born to work."

Carlos didn't view leadership—building relationships that drive results and develop others—as an important form of work. In fact, he didn't view it as work at all. As a result, he paid higher and higher taxes in the form of strained relationships, high staff turnover, and gradual workaholism.

Taxes, obviously, serve as a negative incentive. That is, we are incentivized to avoid or reduce the taxes we pay. On the opposite end of the spectrum, we have dividends. A dividend represents money we are paid, or the reward from an investment. This provides a positive incentive, in that we are motivated not by a fear of loss but by the potential for gain.

People often invest in companies that pay a dividend and then automatically reinvest that additional money to compound their overall investment over time. This is smart financially, and it plays out the same way in the world of relationships.

When Carlos hired me to help him build a better structure in his office, one that would let him focus on higher-order decisions and improve his quality of life in terms of schedule autonomy, we had to start with the values and incentives that specifically guide him. We discussed how people are unique and that he can't lead others the same way he wants to be led unless they are hardwired like him. Few people are.

We started by identifying his goals and values as they apply to the next chapter of his business. We then used those goals and values to form the foundation for his office structure (think org chart, onboarding, expectations, training, evaluation), ensuring that he shifted his focus to clarifying the company vision and goals and developing his team members. Carlos had achieved success not because of his behaviors but in spite of them. He wanted to continue to grow his assets under management and develop others' skill sets, but to do this he had to build relationships and focus on others' behaviors, skills, capacities, and gaps.

What behaviors was he willing to change to get different results? Values. Structure. Communication. Once we clarified these things and he started to hire team members he could trust, the relational dividends quickly started compounding, where team members wanted to do more work, not less. They wanted to build the firm, not maintain it.

The problem is that leaders like Carlos—who are successful *in spite of* something rather than *because of* something—aren't aware of the relationship tax they are creating. They can't see how behaviors are creating a bottleneck that prevents or slows future growth. This approach slowly deteriorates trust and gives life to private resentments, to a culture where people know the boss will do my work, and to a culture of trained helplessness.

At the same time, the Carloses of the world overlook how communication can create a relational dividend, bringing joy, relief, and solutions to team members in need. And remember, unless we specifically ask through data collection, team members keep the taxes and dividends to themselves rather than letting leadership know how they have been impacted.

Root Questions

- Name two ways your workplace behaviors create relational taxes.
- Name two ways your workplace behaviors create relational dividends.
- Write out each of your direct reports' work-style strengths and gaps.
- For the first ten days of a new hire (that you work with), what are you doing to create dividends and limit taxes?

Missing Conversation Quick Facts

CATEGORY	AWARENESS
Missing Conversation	Culture of Relational Taxes or Dividends
What It Does	Allows leaders to understand that they can be successful in spite of something rather than because of it.
Why It Matters	Cultures that intentionally pay relational dividends attract and retain top talent that enhances organizational capacity.

CHAPTER 7

STRATEGY RESIDES IN RESEARCH

"WE JUST WANT TO GROW. INCREASE TOP-LINE revenue. Boost the bottom line. Double sales. Maintain double-digit annual growth." These are typical responses I receive when I ask organizational leaders about their strategy. They focus on the desired outcome—growth—instead of the more challenging topic of *how they will achieve* that growth. At its core, strategy is a game plan for success, a game plan that makes it easy to say yes and no as opportunities arise. If that opportunity doesn't fit the strategic intent, then it should be an easy no. Strategy is *the* framework that simplifies opportunity decisions.

Outside of financial service firms, where the scoreboard is all about making more money, increased revenue and profit margins should be an outcome of doing operational activities more strategically and differently from competitors. The problem is that many leaders skip the important strategic conversation opportunities in favor of quantifying growth goals, because that is a more straight-forward discussion.

Growth goals are essential to the process of strategic planning, but they should only be one part of this overall process. As Michael Porter, the founder of the modern strategy field, reminds us, strategic planning is a process that gives leaders the space for strategic thinking.[15] And to properly discuss company strategy, leaders need to first get clear on what *strategy* means to the team and why they should use it to guide their business decisions. The strategy should be clearly identified, communicated, and nimble enough to flex to the needs and directions of the market.

Strategy is the theoretical part of business. It is planning euphoria, the excitement that emerges from thinking and talking about where the business could go. Depending on the size of your business, it can involve current-state assessments, business-contingency plans, pro forma projections, analytical analyses, workforce planning, SWOT analyses, and of course, market segmentation and demographic discussion. But in small and medium organizations, strategy is often viewed as an annual off-site retreat that ends up focusing on new revenue goals and leaves out the mindset and perspective changes that result from taking our heads out of daily operational decisions and processes and looking around at competitors and customers. While these events are refreshing and momentarily motivating, many of the ideas generated from them are often poorly executed because the ideas are disconnected from the company's comparative and competitive advantages, from its competitors, and from its market economics.

Strategy conversations are where leaders should be thinking with and through their teams, bringing in data about their customers and competitors, talking about how their business is different than others, how they can better serve their customers, and what specific factors create and sustain their competitive advantage. From the strategic planning sessions that I've participated in (but not the ones my firm leads), the focus is more on completing the templates and frameworks that are part of the planning process than actually thinking deeply and differently about one's business. Many leaders get uncomfortable with this process because it requires them to embrace uncertainty, admit not having all the answers, be willing to say "I don't know but we will find out," and treat the process of strategic thinking/talking as a form of necessary action. They aren't aware that strategic thinking is a mindset to be cultivated and brought back from a strategic retreat and planted into daily operational activities.

A crucial but underappreciated idea is that strategy resides in research. Or as the former US Secretary of State James Baker said, "Proper preparation prevents poor performance." [16] Proper preparation can only come from research, from a systematic and rigorous approach to understanding one's current business strengths and weaknesses, especially as they relate to direct competitors and core customers. The fastest way to irrelevance and insolvency is to stop delighting your customers.

You can't engage in strategic thinking, which should be the output of a strategic planning retreat, without the entire leadership team digging into industry and market research. This must be a collaborative team sport like basketball rather than a siloed team sport like golf. It is reasonable to require people to conduct individualized research for their assigned action items, but once the team comes together the ideas can no longer be tied to people; they are now the property of the team. They are the X's and O's the team will use to build the strategic playbook for success.

Root Questions

- Describe your company's current form of strategic planning.
- What's the relationship between strategic thinking and action?
- What is the *value* as compared to the *cost* of temporarily focusing on strategic opportunities instead of daily operational needs?

Missing Conversation Quick Facts

CATEGORY	AWARENESS
Missing Conversation	Strategic Planning Is Really Strategic Thinking and Research
What It Does	Gives leadership teams the opportunity to think deeply and differently about their business, especially as it relates to key competitors and core customers.
Why It Matters	When you stop delighting your customers, you eventually go out of business, and the best way to continually delight your customers over time is to develop flexible strategies through ongoing research and a culture that values strategic mindsets.

CHAPTER 8

ENOUGH

MICHAEL DELL BUILT HIS COMPANY CULTURE AROUND the principle "Pleased But Never Satisfied."[17] He meant that he would show congratulations and excitement when goals were achieved, but that would not satisfy his hunger to improve or grow both himself and his company. He had awareness of his values and integrated them directly into his business as guiding principles. The values served as magnets that attract people who believe in them and repel people who feel the opposite.

That is what an intentionally curated culture is all about. It takes talent, discipline, or both to strike the delicate balance between continuous improvement and constant innovation on the one end, and satisfaction, celebration, and contentment on the other. Spending too much time on one end of the continuum without recognizing the opposite end will lead to burnout or complacency.

Dell's approach to business and life is not for everyone and should be used with caution. The problem with case study and best practice assemblers is that the values, tactics, and strategies in the cases are amazing and clearly drive positive results for some, but if leaders order from that menu without believing those same things in their gut, they are unlikely to drive long-term value creation for their company.

Dell was successful because this value exemplified who he was and is, and he recruited others who felt the same way and who had unique problem-solving skills that he didn't. This enabled him to build a team and company that lived on the cutting edge of development. When you live on the cutting edge, you bleed at times, but that was part of the risk of doing new things and an acceptable part of their culture.

Embracing a unique philosophy like Michael Dell's requires a commitment to vigilant and persistent communication around that principle. Most importantly, it must be a principle or value that is actually lived and felt by the leaders.

Discussing the lived experience or absence of company values as often as possible will maintain momentum, refresh motivation, and prevent the emergence of mediocrity (disguised as accomplishment). A commitment to this type of pillar of excellence relies on an ongoing ability to have difficult conversations around performance standards, accountability, and person/role fit.

To live the company value of being "pleased but never satisfied," a leader can never have *enough* conversations about what the pillar's presence and absence looks like in the workplace. Whereas most of the chapters in this section are about a lack of awareness, Michael Dell was/

is fully aware of what makes his company culture unique and would agree with the founder of modern management, Peter Drucker, who said, "Culture eats strategy for breakfast."[18]

Root Questions

- Describe your reaction to the statement *Culture eats strategy for breakfast.*
- How do you know whether your company values are (a) unique to your organization or (b) generic enough to be copy and pasted onto any corporate business plan?
- How do your organizational values act as magnets, attracting and repelling different types of candidates?
- If you had to pick the top value that guides your organization, what is it, and why?
- Would your leadership team members answer the previous question the same way?

Missing Conversation Quick Facts

CATEGORY	AWARENESS
Missing Conversation	How You Know When You Are Living Your Core Values
What It Does	Discussing and acting on core values every day maintains momentum, refreshes motivation, and prevents the emergence of mediocrity (disguised as accomplishment).
Why It Matters	Authentic and lived values serve as magnets that attract talented people who believe in them and repel people who feel differently about them.

CHAPTER 9

THE THREE BRICKLAYERS

A PARABLE HAS EMERGED OVER THE YEARS THAT TIES back to the famous English architect Christopher Wren's reconstruction of St. Paul's Cathedral in London after it burned down. The story goes that Wren was on-site observing some bricklayers, and he approached them with a simple question: "What are you doing?"

The first bricklayer replied that he was simply working hard to feed his family. The second replied that he was constructing the walls of a church. The third said he was building a kingdom. The truth of the story is less important than its lesson, which revolves around work identity, perspective, and creating meaning in life. In most versions of this story, the first bricklayer was not focused on doing high-quality work, the second bricklayer was doing average or good work, and the third bricklayer was producing high-quality work worthy of excellence. The connection between each man's "why," or sense of work purpose, and his quality of work is an important point.

The first bricklayer's identity and loyalty were tied to his family. That was the perspective that mattered most to him. Laying bricks was a suitable way to exchange his labor for value that kept his family secure. The quality of work was not a factor in how he viewed his tasks, as long as the quality wasn't poor enough to lose the job.

The second bricklayer was tying his identity to a profession, to the occupation of bricklaying and the larger purpose of the actual task at hand, which was—at least that particular day—constructing the walls of a cathedral. He aimed to follow and adhere to professional standards, which could label his work normal or good.

The third bricklayer's perspective was anchored by the most abstract meaning, the idea of building God's kingdom on earth. He was clearly aware of making a small contribution to something much bigger than himself, of belonging to something meaningful far beyond the immediate task at hand. This higher calling, or purpose, compelled him to excellence.

Work, profession, and calling—these are the perspectives the bricklayers brought to their daily labor.

I believe that people who are lucky enough to view their work as part of either a larger profession or as their calling strive to add value in more substantive ways than people who merely view it as a means to put food on the table. It is not a bad perspective to provide sustenance and security for one's family; it is just limited. It prevents a person from identifying and achieving their potential. It is a self-limiting belief wrapped in a security blanket. This is coming from someone whose parents were both workers, strong individual contributors who did great things for the organizations they worked for, but who also did not view their work as a calling or profession. As of this writing, my father is seventy-nine years old and still drives forklifts, packs household items, and builds crates in the furniture-moving business. His calling comes from outside of work, from his roles and volunteer activities he has performed for more than sixty years at his church.

My point is not that every person will naturally infuse their work tasks with mission-driven meanings, but that leaders have the chance to offer a glimpse of that perspective by baking the mission into the culture. They can do that by helping people see how their daily labor connects to something much larger than themselves. Yes, doing this takes time, energy, and strategy, and leaders cannot guarantee that their workforce will adopt the perspective of the third bricklayer. Most won't. But it is human nature and standard psychology for us to want to be a part of something bigger than ourselves, to belong, to contribute to a meaningful cause, to understand how *my* bricks connect to the bigger picture.

When leaders bring the mission to their team and translate activities into mission terms, they increase the chance for this perspective to take root.

Root Questions

- In what ways do you naturally think like the first, second, and third bricklayers?
- How can each of these perspectives be useful to your organization?
- What is left on the table if most of the focus is on the first bricklayer's perspective?
- Have a conversation with your team to discuss whether you should level-up perspectives.

Missing Conversation Quick Facts

CATEGORY	AWARENESS
Missing Conversation	Perspectives and Meanings Matter to Our Work
What It Does	Clarifies the larger purpose or mission that the organization is serving and then uses that understanding to help their team see how individual work connects to the bigger picture.
Why It Matters	Viewing work as part of a larger profession or as a person's calling adds value in more substantive ways than simply viewing it as a means to subside.

CHAPTER 10

CREATIVE SKILLS TRAINING

THERE ARE SOME SKILLS THAT ARE HARD TO TRAIN because capturing the data is difficult.

In the social sciences, for example, the domestic violence dilemma is the idea that we could reduce the occurrence of domestic violence if we could just collect data from a willing group of domestic violence offenders about why they do what they do. That is difficult data to collect for obvious reasons.

A similarly difficult type of data to collect is on how to help police officers identify whether a driver is drunk after they pull someone over. Most police departments train for this by showing videos of actual drunk drivers to new officers and discussing typical behaviors. However, nothing is quite the same as experiencing a scenario firsthand in real life.

While it is possible to predict when drunk drivers are on the roads, it is still no guarantee that police will have the opportunity to learn how to identify and remove one from the streets, keeping streets safer for everyone. But one Florida police department got creative.

The department embraced an unconventional and innovative approach to solving the problem of unreliable DWI/DUI recognition when newer officers pull over citizens. The department invited citizens to the police station and allowed them to consume alcohol until a variety of legal limits were passed, and then had the new officers conduct field sobriety tests on the citizens. The department did not have citizens get behind the wheel, but they did put them through a battery of tests, including walking backwards, marching, and saying the alphabet backwards.

This hands-on, creative approach to skills training was not only effective for the department, it was also entertaining for the involved citizens and useful for their community. Ideas like this are born by thinking about missing conversations, by asking what's absent in an organization's standard procedures or how a process can be improved, and then by being open to whatever ideas emerge. Judging ideas too prematurely guarantees the death of creativity.

Why are new ideas not attempted more often? What keeps people from thinking about, talking about, and trying out creative new solutions to old problems? Most people lack awareness that new ideas can even be created and tried out, often because they are overwhelmed with just completing the work piling up on their desk. But I can think of three main culprits that prevent innovative solutions to old problems:

1. Lack of Courage
2. Lack of Champions
3. Lack of Resources

The first is the most basic and relates to fear and perception, and perhaps a bit of legal risk-based ignorance.[19] Thoughtful organizational leaders are conscious about how their actions are perceived by others, internally and externally to the organization, and this anxiety is heightened when the organization is a public-facing one. The leaders in this police department exhibited courage by moving forward with this creative idea.

Second, these projects need a persistent and well-respected internal champion to shepherd them through the layers of bureaucracy that would typically kill something that doesn't check a pre-defined box. This takes time and energy.

The final barrier to a creative endeavor like citizen field sobriety tests is resource constraints. Organizing any new process, event, or program consumes scarce time and money, even more so when part of a public organization like a police force. The fact that a police department moved forward with such a unique program suggests that the *value* the community received from the program was higher than the program's perceived *costs*. A bonus is that this innovative program led to a great story and additional marketing for the safety of its community.

Root Questions

- What do creative/innovative conversations sound like in your organization?
- When do they occur, and how long are they allowed to unfold?
- What is the most innovative decision, project, or program your company has accomplished in the last two years?
- Would you describe yourself as a catalyst or bottle-neck for creative conversations?

Missing Conversation Quick Facts

CATEGORY	AWARENESS
Missing Conversation	Innovative Solutions for Old Problems
What It Does	Creates new perspectives for challenges that everyone takes for granted.
Why It Matters	Innovative ideas and projects create energy and momentum instead of allowing a lack of courage, lack of internal project champion, or lack of resources to block innovation.

CHAPTER 11

KNOW YOUR ECHO

WHEN THE BOSS IS AROUND, LOOK BUSY. MANY TOP-LEVEL leaders (CEOs, executive directors, owners, founders) subconsciously know their employees and team members alter their behaviors and actions when they enter the room, but it is difficult to fully experience what this is like without collecting data.[20] Systematic data collection can uncover patterns for how people alter their behaviors when different stakeholders are present. The most frequent interaction opportunities for stakeholders across the org chart in organizational settings are meetings, but unfortunately, meetings are often considered a menace because they are poorly conceived and executed.

Leaders put very little strategic thought into designing an effective meeting cadence, meeting structure, and interaction expectations, preferring instead to "wing it." The "winging it" approach to meetings costs companies billions of dollars in wasted time and lost productivity, not to mention decreased team morale and trust.

One recent study showed that for companies of one hundred people, cutting *unnecessary* meetings would save nearly $2.5 million each year. For companies of five thousand people, that savings rises to over $100 million per year.[21] The key is figuring out which meetings are necessary and which aren't, and then creating and expecting an effective meeting culture with standard expectations.

Leaders need to become aware that what they say and how they say it creates a big impact on their teams, even if that impact is not immediately palpable.

To put it another way, leaders need to know their *echo*.

George, the CEO of an agricultural company with $125 million in annual revenue, wanted to improve how his team made decisions, create a more efficient meeting structure, and eliminate unnecessary meetings. My team conducted research including on-site observations, surveys, and interviews to assemble a Current State assessment of the company's meeting culture. Our goal was simple: to understand current meeting norms and processes.

One theme that emerged was crystal clear, and quite uncomfortable: George viewed himself as an extremely *collaborative* leader, yet all his executive peers rated him as a much more *authoritative* leader. He relied on his position to make decisions and regularly dominated meetings where he'd shut down his peers without realizing it, because no one wanted to speak up in the moment (also partially due to the fact that George's family started the business three generations ago).

George was not aware that he was a hammer who saw everything and everyone as nails. He had deep subject matter expertise in the science behind his company's product lineup, and he had overseen the company's expansion to doubling its market share. But his singular communication style was being interpreted as barking orders all day, even when he was trying to explore issues with his team and make decisions collaboratively.

George was not aware of the echo that remained when he left the room, and his direct reports weren't thrilled to offer this unsolicited advice—at least until our diagnostic project gave them the cover of anonymous feedback.

Luckily, George was proactive and concerned with self-improvement, and at the beginning of our project I require all project champions to agree to behavioral change if we learn that they are part of a patterned problem. Not only did he welcome the feedback, but he was stunned by it and wanted to take immediate strides to change. He was appalled that his leadership team and operational teams dreaded meetings that he attended, that they felt he stifled communication rather than encouraged it. Meeting culture at his company had suffered across the board because of it.

With this data, we worked on active-listening behaviors, creating specific meeting structures and interaction norms for a variety of different types of meetings. We also held an executive leadership meeting where George owned up to his past behaviors, apologized (where needed), and asked forgiveness. He followed this up with the same message in his 1:1 meetings.

The conversation he was missing was two-fold: One was an internal conversation around self-awareness of his communication patterns, and this can only be prompted through feedback from others. The second missing conversation was with his team, to discover whether what he perceived as his "collaborative work style" was actually collaborative. We instituted simple pulse checks to ensure the meetings were productive and collaborative moving forward.

Root Questions

- Describe your leadership team's meeting culture: norms, expectations, structures used, typical interactions.
- Rate your level of awareness of your *echo*. In other words, what stories do team members tell about you when you're not in the room, and how do you know?
- How does your echo enhance or impede the meetings you attend?
- In a typical meeting, describe when you normally speak.
- When is the last time you have taken the "pulse" of your meeting culture to determine its level of effectiveness and efficiency?

Missing Conversation Quick Facts

CATEGORY	AWARENESS
Missing Conversation	Self-Awareness of Communication Style in Meetings
What It Does	Enhances a leader's understanding of themselves so they can adjust their style and structure to ensure a productive and energizing meeting culture.
Why It Matters	Meetings constitute a huge time-and-energy commitment in organizational settings, so an inaccurate self-awareness of one's communication style or poorly managed meeting structures are a direct waste of time and money and lead to poor morale.

CHAPTER 12

THE RISK LENS

SOPHIA LISTENED PATIENTLY TO THE GENERAL COUNSEL of her university. The attorney methodically went through an analysis of why the proposed concept—of partnering with regional business owners to support the university's growing eSports program—could be problematic.

After ten minutes of thorough risk analysis of required branding guidelines, action steps for physical injury from slips and falls from community stakeholders being on campus, and the type of in-depth contracts the local business owners would have to sign to protect the university, the general counsel concluded, "We do not believe the reward is worth the risk for this type of partnership."

Sophia, serving as dean of the College of Arts and Sciences, whose role has fiduciary responsibility for the college, asked her general counsel a question and then offered a statement. She asked if in her role as college dean she had the *authority* to initiate the event regardless of these identified risks.

After receiving an affirmative to her question, she thanked the general counsel for their thorough analysis of the legal risks involved with this kind of innovative partnership, as she confirmed her intuition that the attorney had *advisory* authority in this situation, giving Sophia final decision-making power over whether to move forward.

Sophia said that while she appreciated and understood the legal risks, as fiduciary for the college, she had the responsibility for the business risks of the college. With the college in need of revenue due to state funding drying up, all departments were charged with looking for ways to create profit centers, especially in ways that could benefit the university and the community. This opportunity fit that mandate, and she stated that the business risk of passing on this opportunity outweighed the potential legal risks of a partnership.

She viewed the legal risks as reasonable and assigned them a low probability of occurring, concluding her conversation by conveying her confidence that the legal office would draft watertight agreements that would protect the university. She also mentioned she was willing to sign a document saying she believed the business risks outweighed the legal risks. By this point, the attorney was on board with Sophia's approach and said it would not be necessary for her to sign a separate agreement and that they would have the partnership agreements drawn up by the end of the week.

Her approach was masterful and brilliant, turning a potential adversary into an ally. In securing her permission to share this anecdote in the book, Sophia explained she must often choose between the best legal decision and the best business decision. Her counsel helps her understand and make appropriate legal decisions to keep her well within the law and to help protect the university in her business opportunities.

But she must also make business decisions that navigate the business risk. To help with this, she calculates and shares with legal counsel how she will monitor the business risk and how she will respond to a situation should key indicators signal a problem.

Risk management is an important topic that leaders should be aware of, but because this is such a nuanced and specialized field, many leaders without a background in law, insurance, technology, or finance tend to have their confidence shrink during risk-based conversations. This scenario highlights the importance of asking clarifying questions to understand the type of risks involved in a decision, confirming decision rights for who has authority over a decision, and collaboratively approaching how to accept or mitigate identified risks with the team.

For most people, risk entails loss, the unknown, and uncertainty, but it also includes opportunities to innovate, create revenue, grow a business, and build a path of illumination through the darkness of uncertainty. Risk has *odds*, while uncertainty has *unknowns*.[22] And it is always better to make decisions that have probabilities (odds) tied to them than to act from positions of pure uncertainty.

In this case, Sophia had an unusual awareness of a conversation that is missing in far too many organizations: *What is the risk, and who has the decision-making authority?*

Many people would have shriveled under the assertive advice from the general counsel, but Sophia was aware of the university's priorities and her mandate as college fiduciary. Rather than getting defensive, she approached the conversation from a collaborative perspective, viewing the legal counsel as part of her team. She curated the conversation, laying down barriers that guided the discussion in a positive direction. She grew the bamboo in a purposeful way.

The biggest risk would have been forgoing these partnerships, which have turned out to be very lucrative and value-adding for students, for the community, and for the businesses. Sophia's approach to this key conversation is an excellent reminder of the old cliché, *No risk, no reward.*

Root Questions

- How does your company clarify "decision rights"[23] for major decisions (if at all)?
- What does risk mean to you? To your leadership team members?
- In what ways do you incorporate concrete discussions of risk into major decisions?
- How is risk either implicit or explicit in your leadership team discussions?
- How much time is given to talking about risk?

Missing Conversation Quick Facts

CATEGORY	AWARENESS
Missing Conversation	Risk-Reward Analysis and Decision-Making
What It Does	Defines inherent risks and proposed rewards of a potential initiative, and names the person ultimately responsible for weighing the pros and cons and making the final decision whether to move forward.
Why It Matters	Ensures (a) that decisions are made with all relevant information taken into account and all necessary voices being heard; and (b) that the individual responsible for the final decision is known to all and empowered to act.

SECTION 2:

AVOIDANCE

*"A cat never walks across a hot stove twice,
but it doesn't walk across a cold one either."*
—Mark Twain

Many leaders realize they should engage in critical-but-difficult conversations to enhance their organization, yet they knowingly choose to avoid them. Conversational avoidance leads to a variety of problems in morale/culture, trust reduction, strategic stop-and-starts, and operational misfires. When leaders *knowingly* avoid key conversations, they are leading from weakness and fear and eventually guarantee inconsistent goal execution. Missing conversations because of avoidance immediately leads to negative consequences and models poor workplace behaviors. There's always at least one other person who is aware that a topic should be discussed but is instead being avoided. This isn't a recipe for growth, winning, and achievement.

Conversational avoidance that results from personal fear and anxiety or potential business risks is a formula for frozen market share. It leads to missed opportunities and poor internal organizational communication.

CHAPTER 13

NICE GUYS LISTEN LAST

PERSONAL TRAITS AND BEHAVIORS THAT ARE ADMIRED and desired have an interesting effect in the workplace. Because of the weighting we each assign to behaviors we like, we tend to overlook or downplay behaviors we find problematic. Frederick Hertzberg created a model about what motivates humans built around two areas: motivators and hygiene factors.[24] He elaborated that people have complex thoughts about an experience based on the elements that satisfy them and the elements that cause dissatisfaction. He coined the terms *satisfiers* and *dissatisfiers*, where people can be both satisfied and dissatisfied with an experience, company, or service simultaneously. Companies should learn how to understand both sets of motivating factors and how customers and employees weight them.

Returning to my friend Jake from earlier in the book, we can see that his lack of listening (dissatisfier) was outweighed by his politeness, likability, and niceness (satisfier). His niceness caused people to tolerate his argumentativeness because the way he argued his ideas was not overly aggressive. But it did prevent collaborative dialogue. This was both beneficial and detrimental because while it allowed Jake to articulate ideas for the opportunity of moving them forward (and he is very persuasive), it also neglected others' ideas that might have been just as beneficial to the problem.

I'm certainly not implying that all "nice" people are poor listeners; I'm just saying that having a desired quality like niceness can outweigh other undesirable qualities and limit personal, team, and company growth.

Through coaching, consulting, and executive mediation, I witness my clients give more latitude to their nice employees when it comes to poor performance and productivity dips. It is harder to hold these people accountable *because* they are nice, because the evaluators don't want to hurt their feelings since the nice person is seemingly concerned with others' feelings.[25] But Shane Parrish, author of *Clear Thinking*, reminds us that there is a difference between being *kind* and being *nice*. In the workplace, you should strive for kindness rather than niceness. A kind person will tell you what is difficult to hear because they care about you and want to see you improve, whereas a nice person will avoid that conversation because it is a sensitive topic.

Kindness leads to cultivated growth; niceness leads to stagnation and atrophy.

Kindness is bamboo curation; niceness is out-of-sight invasiveness.

In the episode called "The Bubble" of the television show *30 Rock,* the main character, Liz Lemon, is attracted to one of her neighbors, a charming and handsome doctor played by Jon Hamm.[26] Over the course of the episode, you learn that Hamm's good looks hypnotize people into ignoring his flaws, namely his lack of intelligence and common sense. For instance, his character cannot conduct the Heimlich maneuver despite him being a doctor, and he is a terrible tennis player despite being a tennis coach. People instead put him on a pedestal and infuse all his behaviors and choices with positive meaning because of the shining light of his handsome demeanor. This type of halo effect is beneficial to someone until it isn't, until their positive-trait bubble pops and they must face reality.

I see this pattern in my charismatic clients. The charisma masks unpleasant traits and behaviors that either people ignore, overlook, or consciously redefine to a more positive meaning. This latter form of self-gaslighting is extremely unproductive for teams and organizations because it presents a limited view of reality, allowing innovative solutions to remain undiscussed, leading to less value creation, and delighting fewer customers.

Root Questions

- Discuss whether individuals who are perceived as nice in your organization are required to adhere to the same performance standards as others.
- Describe the point at which being nice/agreeable is problematic on a leadership team.
- What tools does your team use to shift out of agreeableness and into effective confrontation and structured disagreement?

Missing Conversation Quick Facts

CATEGORY	AVOIDANCE
Missing Conversation	Acknowledging Attitudes That Stifle Accountability
What It Does	Allows team to discuss traits or behaviors that people avoid, overlook, or consciously redefine to a more positive meaning.
Why It Matters	Avoiding an uncomfortable conversation about a particular problematic behavior will create a double standard that penalizes high performers and instead rewards that particular behavior.

CHAPTER 14

ANGRY ELEPHANTS

IT'S IMPORTANT TO GO ELEPHANT HUNTING NOW AND then in the workplace. This type of behavior should not be relegated to crisis, change, or strategic implementations; it should be a regularly occurring part of a healthy workplace.

By *elephant hunting*, I mean having the vigilance and courage to discuss the difficult topic in the room that no one wants to address or that no one else sees. The purpose is not to kill the elephant, the goal is to:

1. Capture it.
2. Nurture it.
3. Release it back into the wild.

In *capturing* the elephant, the team does what is necessary to address an important and difficult topic, maintaining the appropriate sensitivity when bringing it up and helping peers save face as much as possible.

By *nurturing* the elephant, I mean giving the topic the proper depth and sufficient substance when talking through it with stakeholders. A quick mention of a challenging topic is not enough. Elephants don't fill up on appetizers; they need a five-course meal of a discussion.

Releasing it back into the wild means being able to breathe a sigh of relief, check the topic off your list, and move on to the next priority.

When uncertainty drives us into anxiety, people fill in gaps with unflattering assumptions. I was advising an architecture, engineering, and construction organization through a complex change process that was transitioning from a traditional holding company legal structure with six decentralized, autonomously operating business entities to a centralized operating company structure, where all support business functions would be centralized. In addition, this organization with $225 million in annual revenue was also looking to carve out profit centers by combining services across entities. This was a challenging change process because the strategic change leaders were also the heads of the operating centers, so they had to keep the lights on and devote time to the restructuring process.

While there would be fewer CEOs on the new organizational chart, none of their compensation was going to change, only their titles, status, and authority. But for most people, those things are just as important (if not more) than compensation. The leaders who were shuffled out of well-defined and traditional positions of authority did not take the news well.

The image below shows the main reasons that people resist organizational change, and they all relate to common patterns in human nature. It requires *SACRIFICE*:

STATUS
AUTHORITY
COMPENSATION
RESPECT
INDEPENDENCE
FOCUS
INTENT
CALLING
EXCELLENCE

Figure 5. People resist organizational change because these factors shift.

These topics are hard to discuss. Yet the more *difficult* they are to talk about, the more *important* they are to talk about and the sooner those conversations should occur. That is the advice I always give to clients.

So, what is the common strategy during change projects?

Sadly, the most-used strategy in these situations is to avoid the conversation and hope the issue will go away or the person will resolve the internal dissonance on their own.

A change process of the magnitude my client was going through usually takes two or three years (for well-resourced companies) to complete a full implementation. There were a lot of long-tenured team members across the decentralized organizations who were loyal to their operating entity but not to the overall enterprise brand. They were operators, not strategic thinkers. And their organizational identity was changing.

It was clear we needed to have direct conversations about business function redundancies, service synergies to carve out new revenue, and a deeper analysis of which leaders would remain in leadership seats. But the key leaders instead chose to punt the discussions for twelve months, which kept everyone in a fog of uncertainty longer than most of them could bear. As a result, a few great team members left the company for greener pastures—which, incidentally, were mostly with competitors. Instead of addressing the elephant in the room, the executives leading the transition thought it would be easier in the short term to avoid these conversations. But all that did in the long term was give their competitors a leg up by essentially gift wrapping for them their most skilled, experienced team members. Oops.

While the client couldn't have guaranteed these leaders would have stuck around through the restructuring regardless, they would have had a much better chance if they had engaged in the difficult conversations earlier in the change process. Instead, they lost key players and burned bridges.

The aftermath of an angry elephant is never pretty.

Root Questions

- How often do you make it a priority to ask, "What are we not talking about?" or "What are we avoiding?"
- When a tense topic emerges that everyone knows about, what is common practice in your organization: discuss it immediately, discuss it eventually, or avoid discussing it altogether? How effective has that been?
- How might individual team members' emotions prevent important conversations at your company?

Missing Conversation Quick Facts

CATEGORY	AVOIDANCE
Missing Conversation	The Elephant in the Room
What It Does	Gives an important and difficult topic the proper depth and sufficient substance to understand key stakeholders' thoughts and perspectives.
Why It Matters	Avoiding difficult topics negatively impacts the culture, rewards poor behavioral patterns, and creates distrust, which all lead to less-than-optimal results.

CHAPTER 15

WALKING ON EGGSHELLS

WHEN LEADERS WALK ON EGGSHELLS AROUND PEOPLE, it's a problem. The issue is that we have come up with all kinds of stories we sell ourselves to rationalize why we do it. By avoiding direct and candid conversations with our team members and peers, we are doing them, our relationship with them, and the company a disservice.

If you are spending *unreasonable* amounts of time engaging in message strategy to have conversations with peers or direct reports, you are probably walking on eggshells. That is not beneficial for skill development, relationships based on honest and useful feedback, or the consistent achievement of excellence.

We walk on eggshells for demographic and personal-identity reasons as often as we do for performance-issue and skill-deficiency reasons. Both cases set all parties up for suboptimal communication and cultivate a culture of distrust.

Walking on eggshells around someone also shifts the focus onto individual interests and away from team and company goals. While this can be important for a short-term situation, it is not an effective long-term strategy for a productive culture. More importantly, we train others that this is an acceptable part of organizational culture—and it will eventually be acknowledged and abused.

Eggshell environments become so scrubbed of emotion and honesty that they begin to feel sterile, bland, and sanitized—hardly the recipe for building interpersonal team trust.

One of my coaching clients, a successful attorney named Briley, had more than fifteen years' experience as an insurance defense attorney. Briley was brilliant at constructing case narratives, and she was promoted to lead a team that included several male team members who were all older than she was. Another layer of complexity is that she went from working with peers to managing them. This is never easy, but it's rarely directly addressed.

Briley began to change her communication style with these team members, trying to convince herself it was out of respect for their experience. The truth is, though, she was being condescending toward them. She assumed they would not be able to deal with direct conversations about poor performance when it was coming from a younger, female colleague.

She wasn't showing her direct reports respect; she was projecting her internal baggage onto them.

When she changed her perspective and communicated with honesty and from a position of helpfulness, her relationships improved. Better yet, their performance improved because she clarified workplace performance standards for them that they had been consistently missing. Briley took it a step further by admitting the tension she felt in managing former peers, and she showed genuine respect for them by encouraging them to push back and challenge her whenever she wasn't being clear.

We can't ignore the fact that people have different levels of sensitivity. However, when you are on the same team, you must give others the benefit of the doubt, grab two minutes of courage, and share what you're thinking and why you're hesitant. Most of the time, this honesty will be appreciated and reciprocated. If not, at least you learn where people stand.

The only thing eggshell environments consistently create is a rotten culture.

Root Questions

- In what ways do you walk on eggshells around people, choosing to avoid sensitive topics because of issues of difference that make you uncomfortable?
- How common is it for your team members to do this?
- Describe a situation when walking on eggshells has led to a useful solution for a relationship or your company.

Missing Conversation Quick Facts

CATEGORY	AVOIDANCE
Missing Conversation	Walking on Eggshells
What It Does	Is beneficial to skill development, relationships based on honest and useful feedback, and the consistent achievement of excellence.
Why It Matters	Eggshell environments become so scrubbed of emotion and honesty that they begin to feel sterile, bland, and sanitized—hardly the recipe for building interpersonal team trust or driving innovative solutions.

CHAPTER 16

THE IMPLIED YES

THE TWO MOST IMPORTANT LETTERS FOR ANY LEADER TO master are N-O.

For a person who sits in a position of authority in an organizational setting, *no* is one of the most strategic answers they can give. Unfortunately, *no* is also one of the most misunderstood words in the English language because of its somewhat negative connotation. Most people don't like hearing the word when they ask someone a question. We often even shy away from asking questions in the first place because we're scared of someone's *no*. But it doesn't have to be this way if you have a deeper understanding of what this word can mean when used strategically.

When a colleague approaches us with an idea to pursue, a project to vet, or a market to study, we might oblige to avoid offending them or out of fear of burning a bridge. This is especially common for managers and directors with less than three years of experience leading teams. They think they are letting their teams down if they say no, and of course, it creates a small feeling of power when we accomplish work tasks that help others out.

Some inexperienced leaders will say *not yet*, creating the impression that at some point in the future the idea will find its legs. That may feel kinder to us in the moment, but it actually hurts the other person by giving them false hope that your *not yet* might someday become a *yes*—even when you know that will never happen.

It is rare for a new leader to say right off the bat, "No, this doesn't fit our current strategy." But the truth is, that is the kindest answer we can give much of the time. Would it be better to keep your answer vague, which in turn causes the other person or team to waste precious time trying to perfect a strategy you know from the outset will not work? How is wasting the team's or individual's time a kinder option than simply saying a clear, direct *no*?

The larger problem is that the power of *no* is rarely baked into strategic plans.[27]

Two of the top reasons companies don't achieve their goals are that (a) they are pursuing too many goals at once or (b) their goal-achievement efforts aren't backed by any strategy.[28] Pursuing seven or eight different strategic objectives might look good on paper—and it surely makes the executive team smile with pride—but the inability to home in on what's most important actually indicates leaders aren't acting as strategically as they think.

What is the top priority? Many leaders can't answer that question with certainty, so they end up spreading their resources too thin and mistake mediocrity for excellence. What's worse is that this redefinition of success— by lowering the bar—is accompanied by built-in excuses for why the goals were not achieved. These take the form of internal rationalizations, like losing a key person; and external reasons, like lingering inflation.

If your leadership team is suggesting your company pursue more than five objectives or goals per quarter, that is a sign your team has not mastered the fine art of *no*.

Every *no* should lead to more time and energy devoted to your highest-priority projects that move your company in the direction of your mission, or what I call your *implied yes*.

There are two missing conversations in this scenario:

First, your team is missing an alignment[29] conversation to gain consensus about what bad, average, good, excellent, and elite goal achievement looks like.

Second, you didn't discuss the range of common excuses that are unacceptable responses if the goals are not hit.

With so many objectives being pursued at once, is your team cohesively aligned with a true north, or are your individual leaders headed in the direction that best fits their business unit or department?

This is why having a top-line strategic intent that can be summoned like a battle cry is so essential—it serves as a filter for the goal-achievement process: setting, valuing, and resetting. As Steve Jobs was fond of discussing, he was most proud of the projects that Apple said *no* to, giving the company the ability to laser-focus on its ability to unleash its *yes* on the projects, opportunities, and innovations that mattered most to its mission.

Root Questions

- How easy or difficult is it for you to harness the positive power of *no*? Why?
- What is your company's *implied yes* every time you turn down a new opportunity?
- In what ways does saying *no* make you uncomfortable, like you are letting others down?
- How do you think the previous question applies to your team members?
- Name two ways you can be more strategic and thoughtful about saying *no*.

Missing Conversation Quick Facts

CATEGORY	AVOIDANCE
Missing Conversation	When to Say *No*
What It Does	Leads to more time, energy, and oversight devoted to your highest-priority projects that move your company in the direction of your *implied yes* (e.g., the mission).
Why It Matters	Saying yes to too many opportunities leads to a redefinition of success—by lowering the bar—accompanied by built-in excuses for why the goals were not achieved.

CHAPTER 17

EFFORT AS TALENT

GRAVEYARDS ARE FULL OF TALENTED PEOPLE WHO didn't have the discipline to focus their efforts in the direction of those natural talents. This isn't meant to be a slight on anyone who didn't take their natural talents as far as they could; it's more of an observation about a fact of human nature.

We are slaves to inertia. Just as an object at rest will tend to remain at rest, a person who is good at a task will tend to remain (simply) good at that task without additional effort. Many leaders avoid talking about effort in the workplace because they believe it is hard to measure, so they opt not to discuss it at all. It is the rare person who is skilled at the process of effort itself, whose very talent is effort. This unique concept—effort as a type of talent—was developed by Dr. Robert Furey[30] in his wonderful book, *The Art of Affirmation.*

In his former role as a practicing psychologist and behavioral therapist for at-risk youth, Dr. Furey began to see a pattern: Certain people are skilled at strenuous exertion regardless of the task. These individuals seem to have a natural inclination toward self-discipline, grit, and persistence that is often lacking in others. Think of the most celebrated people in the modern world, scientists like Albert Einstein and Carl Sagan; athletes like Michael Jordan, Kobe Bryant, and Serena Williams; entrepreneurs and builders like Elon Musk (SpaceX, Tesla, Neuralink), Jack Dorsey (Block, Twitter), and Sarah Blakely (Spanx). They all exhibit effort as talent.

Warren Buffett's recently deceased partner at Berkshire Hathaway, Charlie Munger, would most certainly have agreed with Dr. Furey, that *consistent effort over long periods of time* is the key differentiator in life. On the other end of the spectrum, the rarest people have so much talent in multiple areas that they wear themselves out trying to spread their efforts across all their spheres of talent. Much like wild bamboo, the invasiveness of their organic talents continues to grow but in an untended manner, spreading at a whim with no structures to guide it. Efforts are eventually extinguished with these individuals as well. They burn out. Elite performers do the opposite, focusing their talents and efforts into a single area and cultivating their best work.

For elite performers in sports, art, science, and business, there are multiple talent layers that must coexist, and the most important layer is consistent effort. But this is also the layer that society prefers to avoid, instead desiring the illusion that these elite performers simply have natural talents that propel them and cement their spot in the history books.

As Friedrich Nietzsche teaches in his book *Human, All Too Human*, thinking like that is actually our ego speaking, our security blanket trying to let ourselves off the hook for not achieving greatness. Our sense of self-worth feels better when we explain away greatness in others as "genius" or "God-given talent" instead of sustained hard work over the long haul that led to their mastery. While there is truth to natural physical and cognitive talents and traits, the people we choose to tell stories about are the ones who embrace the grind, who make *effort* their goal, and who laser-focus their efforts over time. They are constantly striving to add more effort than their last performance, in essence competing against their most recent effort level.

The dedication and self-discipline to keep improving, to keep striving, to push through pain is what sets the elite apart from the excellent, the .01 percent from the 1 percent. The pain they overcome can be physical, mental, social, or emotional, but one thing is certain: Elite performers in all fields have mastered their *no* to relentlessly pursue their *yes*. Their *effort-as-talent* approach to life requires it.

Root Questions

- How does your leadership team account for effort in the workplace?
- What is your team's most common response when pain emerges, such as through financial loss or emotional tension?
- What are the most important natural talents to the success of your organization?
- How could you apply the effort-as-talent concept in your organization?

Missing Conversation Quick Facts

CATEGORY	AVOIDANCE
Missing Conversation	Consistent Effort Is Talent
What It Does	Draws attention to the fact that consistent, long-term effort toward a single goal is a key differentiator of success.
Why It Matters	Prevents us from explaining away greatness in our competitors and instead compels us to achieve it through our own sustained efforts.

CHAPTER 18

VULNERABILITY

WHEN YOU AVOID HAVING AN IMPORTANT CONVERSA-tion, you are forgoing opportunities in the form of intimate connections, where you create authentic, natural, and organic closeness with another person. If the conversational avoidance is conscious, it often stems from fear, an unwillingness to be vulnerable,[31] to give up control and let others see you for who you really are. And by sacrificing your self-expression through skipping meaningful conversations, you close off paths to personal creativity, relational connection, and organizational innovation.

Every time I facilitate high-stakes leadership meetings—strategic planning sessions, board meetings, executive conflict, diagnostic problem-solving—each person is required to commit out loud to (a) say what they mean and mean what they say; (b) be open to growth and different perspectives; and (c) give me permission to move the conversation forward when unproductive tension and conflict emerge. I call them the Conversational

Commitments. Teams are always amazed by how deep they can go and how direct they can be once they commit to these things. They find that they can say things to each other that they never thought possible.

I recently facilitated an all-day leadership team meeting for a home goods manufacturing company, where the team reviews its goals and strategic plan, and then engages in problem-solving. They do this quarterly and agreed that they get along very well. The company is growing and recently added a new location, where they plan to ramp up production.

At one point in the meeting, I asked everyone to write down the level of trust they feel the team has, instead of just asking people to shout it out.[32] The general manager ranked 10/10 and assumed everyone else would too. He was wrong. The scores ranged from 10 to 5, with the most frequent ranking being 6.

The surprise and concern were apparent on his face, so I got permission to pivot the conversation to the reasons behind the rankings. This led to an hour-long discussion about ways to improve their team culture and communication practices, including admitting when they felt wronged by each other. Air was cleared. Trust was re-established. No one would have wanted to dig into this type of discussion, even though many of the members felt the need to do so. They avoided it because they weren't the top-level leader and because they didn't want to look "petty." The outcome of this discussion was a new goal focusing on culture development at the team and company level, something that everyone felt was lacking but no one ever dared to bring up. It was a big win for everyone.

While organizations can take steps to create environments that allow for intimacy to naturally emerge, it still takes courage and initiative to make it happen.

I love the "inspired by a true story" movie *We Bought a Zoo*. The main character's wife passes away from a health tragedy at a young age, and he changes his entire life by buying a zoo with his kids. At one point, his teenage son is questioning whether he should talk to a girl he likes, and the father says, "You know, sometimes all you need is twenty seconds of insane courage. Just literally twenty seconds of just embarrassing bravery. And I promise you, something great will come of it."[33]

Twenty seconds of insane courage. Think of all the things that wouldn't have happened if people had lacked courage to kick them off: flourishing relationships, passion projects, startup companies, career transitions. If our ancestors lacked twenty seconds of insane courage the world would look very different today.

When it comes to avoiding difficult conversations in a workplace, I'm not even encouraging *insane* courage; I'm suggesting trying to conjure up a reasonable amount of audacity to have the missing conversation. But we often prefer to focus on the peripheral choices at the peril of the main choice.

We will preoccupy ourselves with comfortable seating, lighting, music, temperature, smells, and food. While these can be key ingredients to enable a fulfilling and vulnerable conversation, they aren't the main course. It takes human action to create a conversation. We can have all the ingredients laid out in front of us and still do nothing with them. Reading a recipe doesn't cure hunger.

If you meet someone new and feel a kinship with them but then choose not to say anything or act on it, you cut off a path that could have led to something amazing. By not expressing gratitude when others do nice things for us, we incrementally increase the callousness around our hearts. While you shouldn't share every intimate thought that crosses your mind in the workplace, you should at least move the needle from *never* sharing to *sometimes* sharing.

Root Questions

- Rate the level of vulnerability on your leadership team from 0 to 10. Explain your rating.
- When your team has important meetings, do you work with a skilled facilitator to focus on creating an engaging discussion, or do you expect members to take on multiple roles?
- Within the last two weeks, what is the most courageous conversation you have had in the workplace?

Missing Conversation Quick Facts

CATEGORY	AVOIDANCE
Missing Conversation	Expressing Vulnerable Ideas
What It Does	Replaces unproductive tension and conflict with increased trust, thereby improving the organizational culture and communication.
Why It Matters	By concealing how we truly feel about things out of fear, we close off paths to personal creativity, relational connection, and organizational innovation.

CHAPTER 19

COMMIT TO THE CASE

MY WIFE AND I WERE RECENTLY WORKING WITH ONE OF our banking partners, updating our individual accounts to place them in the name of our family trust. This institution happens to be one of the big five banks in the US, one of the so-called "too big to fail" banks, and certainly has a complex corporate and bureaucratic structure. As one might expect, we ran into some administrative snags trying to get their systems to communicate and convert our different accounts to the trust. The personal banker we were working with was very friendly and patient but clearly not someone who could solve our issue, as he did not have signature authority.

He picked up on the fact that I was beginning to lose some patience (let's hope Dr. Furey doesn't find out) because we were ninety minutes into what was *supposed* to be a thirty-minute task. He apologized and said with confidence, "I know you have things to do, and I want to get you guys on your way, so I tell you what I am going to do for you. I am placing this in our 'Commit to the Case' program." I actually laughed a bit out loud when he said it, and I immediately felt bad.

I asked him what that meant, and he said it basically meant he would shepherd our request through the bank's systems until the problem was solved. I thanked him for the explanation—even though all I could think about was how absurd it was to have an entirely separate process for what essentially came down to *doing his job until it is done.*

This experience left me wondering about what happens to everyone else's issues. You know, the unlucky folks who don't make the cut of getting into the Committing to the Case program.

Company growth and success usually entail additional bureaucracy, redundant processes, and overlapping authority systems. A byproduct of bureaucratic growth is that without the appropriate strategies and conversations, an impersonal, informal, pass-the-buck culture will emerge without anyone thinking of it that way. A jungle of bamboo stifling what should be a simple business transaction.

Bloat.

Someone else's problem.

"Not my skill set."

Bureaucratic bloat[34] persists when no single person "owns" a case through to completion, when everything is part of a process or system in which cases are tossed around to different departments like a game of hot potato.

The notion of "committing to the case" is simply being accountable for the work on your desk. If the task is truly below your pay grade, hand it off appropriately but then follow up to ensure the problem gets solved.[35]

Delegation. Oversight. Follow-up. Three quaint concepts that are rarely celebrated and often forgotten but that are part of a high-quality operation.

Root Questions

- Describe situations where you might be passing the buck but instead convince yourself that you're delegating.
- Have a conversation about what processes matter most for your team and which are process for process's sake.
- What are the cases where delegation makes sense?
- What problems hit your desk that you should not be solving (e.g., low priority, low value, low impact)?

Missing Conversation Quick Facts

CATEGORY	AVOIDANCE
Missing Conversation	Commit to the Right Amount of Rules
What It Does	Encourages individuals to take ownership of a problem from start to finish.
Why It Matters	Creates an ownership culture that thrives on problem completion rather than problem handoff.

CHAPTER 20

TERMINATE, TOLERATE, OR DEVELOP

I WORK WITH A LOT OF CLIENTS WHO HAVE LONGTIME, loyal employees whose productivity has begun to sag. The business leaders are then faced with what to do in these emotionally complex situations.

In most cases, these employees have been faithful team members over the years, with many even making life-altering decisions like moving their families across the country for the company. But once leaders start talking to me about this situation, the reality is that the individual has either stopped adding value on a regular basis, or worse, has become counterproductive to goal achievement or company culture. This is a challenging situation, as many of my clients took part in the hiring process of this person, have worked with them for several decades, or have a personal relationship in addition to the work relationship.

The most common way people deal with these situations is to avoid them.

But this is *never* an intelligent solution.

To help my clients work through the difficult retention conversations, my team developed a tool called Intentional Retention that brings out quantitative and qualitative insights about a person. By going through this process with a leader or leadership team, the retention decision becomes clear on whether to respectfully *terminate* (with a fair severance), *tolerate* the lack of productivity (rarely a good option), or *develop* this individual's skills. If they land on the third option, professional development, I work with leaders to create a custom performance-improvement plan with clear milestones that need to be achieved to retain employment. I help them create benchmarks and "trip wires" so everyone is on the same page regarding behavioral progress.

A *trip wire* is a decision tool that alerts us to an action we should or shouldn't take once the wire is tripped. It can take the form of "if *this* then *that* logic." For example, if a leadership team member doesn't start with questions when working with his peers (instead starting with his own proposed solution), they won't be allowed to participate in key meetings. The consequence should, of course, be right-sized to the situation and culture, but the point is that we need to clarify the problematic behavior, the expected change, and the positive and negative consequences of behavioral change.

People don't want to draw lines in the sand when personal relationships and emotions complicate subpar productivity and poor attitudes. The great thing about lines in the sand is that they can change over time, or we can erase them as people improve. At their core, these lines are about honoring our commitments to each other in the workplace. Our Intentional Retention tool helps separate the personal from the organizational and allows clients to quantify and qualify the value that a team member adds. This removes a layer of emotionality from difficult decisions. Think of these discussions as a form of pruning that keeps the overall health of the organization vibrant and growing in the right direction.

Retention conversations involving long-term employees and leadership team members tend to be avoided as long as possible, growing a system of underground resentment and anxieties, because people usually don't have useful data to support their instincts or make the case for what is best for the employee, the team, and the company. Due to the lack of data, people then choose to tolerate substandard behaviors out of a sense of misplaced loyalty, overlooking the damage this does to their company standards and to the rest of the team who are striving for productivity.

The only thing high performers hate more than not being properly challenged is seeing the leaders tolerate others' habitual low performance. Tolerating unproductive behavior (performance or attitude[36]) regardless of how long someone has been with a company is never a good decision. The best option, though not always easy, is to collect the data needed to make an informed and fair decision.

Root Questions

- How does your team measure the impact to the organization when a team member isn't pulling their weight?
- Describe your comfort level with telling longtime employees or leadership team members that there are issues with their performance or their attitude.
- On average, how long do you tolerate problematic patterns of behavior before talking about them?

Missing Conversation Quick Facts

CATEGORY	AVOIDANCE
Missing Conversation	Terminate, Tolerate, or Develop
What It Does	Clarifies a retention decision on whether to respectfully *terminate* (with a fair severance), *tolerate* a lack of productivity, or *develop* an individual's skills.
Why It Matters	Removes a layer of emotionality from difficult decisions by separating the personal from the organizational and focusing on the value that a team member adds.

CHAPTER 21

INERTIA HIDES FEAR

"H E'S A GOOD EMPLOYEE. WELL, HE *CAN BE* A GOOD employee. I mean, he gets the major things done when I need him to."

This was what one of my coaching clients said to me about one of her direct reports when I probed her during a bench-strength discussion. She explained that this employee is extremely intelligent and skilled in a narrow swim lane but causes grief for everyone he works with and can be condescending to people who can't keep up with his analysis (which is most people). I asked if this was a behavior she would tolerate if he didn't excel in that narrow swim lane, and she instantly responded with no.

I challenged her to define the exact type of value this person added to the team and the type of problems that he was creating. I also asked about any formal performance plans, coaching, and other interventions that she had used to address or correct his behaviors and set expectations. She said that nothing formal had yet occurred but that she had made several one-off comments to him over the last two years about his condescending attitude. She did think that two key employees left because of him, but she had no data from exit interviews to confirm her hunch.

I finally asked, "What is the real challenge here?"

She replied, "If he isn't willing to change, then I will either have to learn the software that he's an expert on or find someone else who is. I don't have time for either of those things right now."

I asked, "If one of your direct reports made a talent decision based on that same rationale, would you think their decision was a healthy approach for a business, or would you coach them on better ways to handle it?"

Realizing how obvious the solution to her problem was, she declared, "I am going to create a formal improvement plan with clear expectations and coach him for three months on the plan. If it isn't working by then, we will either help him find a better role in the company or I will terminate him."

Prior to this discussion, this otherwise-insightful leader hadn't realized she was making a daily *choice* to accept the pain and misery of working with a non-collaborative, semi-valuable team member who caused friction with other team members. Why? Because of inertia. She did not want to take on more work for herself (technical work that she didn't enjoy), she did not want to backfill an important position, and she feared the change.

When you are faced with a challenging talent decision in the workplace that involves potentially shuffling around the team, ask yourself: *Would I want my direct reports to make decisions like this with their teams?*

If it's an operational challenge, ask, *Am I delaying the inevitable by kicking the can down the road, or am I looking to solve the root problem?*

For strategic decisions, visualize how much more efficient your team and company would be if you pursued optimal solutions that caused a brief interruption at first but ultimately created less work for everyone. The only people that would not support that approach probably shouldn't be working at your company in the first place.

If inertia—the fear of change, failure, rejection, or regret—is holding you back from making challenging decisions, look in a mirror and ask yourself out loud, "Is this inertia leading us to excellence or taking us further from where we want to go?"

Root Questions

- In what ways does inertia prevent your team from succeeding?
- Describe the tools and motivational techniques you personally use to escape the pull of inertia.
- How can inertia be useful in your organization?

Missing Conversation Quick Facts

CATEGORY	AVOIDANCE
Missing Conversation	Where Does Inertia Hold Us Back
What It Does	Examines decisions from the lens of inertia to help determine whether the team is swimming toward excellence or merely treading water.
Why It Matters	Accepting the pain and misery of working with a non-collaborative, semi-valuable team member or poorly designed product or service is a choice.

CHAPTER 22

DISEASE TO PLEASE AND GROUPTHINK

A COMMON PATTERN I SEE ACROSS ALL LEVELS OF AN organization is taking friendliness to an extreme. At its root, this is hardwired into most of us as the social instinct—the desire to be liked, or as I like to call it, the *disease to please.*

This is a difficult behavioral pattern to overcome, because you obviously don't want to go too far the other way and become a jerk, distant, or an overly independent problem solver. It's a fine line to balance, especially for newer managers and executives.

Anytime someone is promoted to the next level on the org chart, you'll tend to see the disease to please rear its head. The fear of not being liked or not being respected will eventually morph into imposter syndrome, where we start to question if we are worthy of a seat at the table.

The disease to please is a rogue form of relationship building that hides our true feelings and skills in favor of what we think is socially acceptable in a new setting.

The higher up the org chart, the more problematic this behavior. This is because there's more responsibility with the decisions made at the top of the chart; they have a wider impact across an organization. When people have to make decisions that affect an entire company or an entire business unit, blindly following our disease to please leads to bad decisions. It causes us to rely too much on consensus-based decision-making, trying not to step on anyone's toes and focusing too much on people's feelings and sensitivities. This is the opposite of leading.

I want to be clear that I am not suggesting being callous or communicating in a way that disregards people's emotions. But I am saying that you need to keep in mind the results you're trying to achieve and the decision-making or consensus mechanism with which you're trying to make a decision.

Sometimes consensus isn't needed and pleasing everyone is not part of the program. And oftentimes widespread agreement can actually be a symptom of groupthink,[37] a nefarious but pleasant-sounding malady that leads groups to believe they are making sound decisions when they really aren't.

The disease to please and its groupthink partner announce themselves wherever group members self-censor for the good of the group, prefer not to rock the boat or go against the grain, and do everything possible to create the illusion of agreement. These groups strive to display a feeling of invulnerability, always masking the disagreement and uncertainty lurking just below the surface. These symptoms of poor decision-making create errors and invite unnecessary risks. Poor results and crushed confidence are also casualties of the disease to please and groupthink.

One of my coaching partners, Dominic, worked for a fast-scaling information technologies company, growing at a 100 percent compound annual growth rate for four years in a row. They also went from fifteen employees to more than 150 in four years.

Dominic's promotion was a clear-cut example of *the Peter Principle*,[38] which describes when a person is promoted beyond their level of competence. While this sounds negative, it isn't. It occurs when companies promote high performers from an individual contributor position to a position they're less skilled at, which usually involves managing and leading others instead of completing individual work tasks and goals. Think of the top-performing salesperson now having to lead the sales team. Those are vastly different roles, and yet many leaders often assume the skills from one role will transfer to the other.

For example, recent researchers have found that high-performing sales employees are more likely to be promoted and perform poorly as managers, because their sales skills do not translate to coaching, managing, leading, and holding others accountable.[39]

Dominic was an extremely talented programmer who wrote clean and efficient code. He had built a wide technical skill set and could solve any kind of technical problem—and he took pride in his ability to help his peers solve their technical problems. Unsurprisingly, he eventually got promoted to Chief Information Officer and then Chief Technology Officer of this organization. However, his technical prowess did not naturally translate into managing teams, growing younger leaders, exhibiting emotional intelligence, or having empathy. As a result, his strategy for dealing with his leadership deficiencies was trying to please everyone.

This might work in the short term, such as with a single project or in the first few weeks of a new job, but it's hardly a long-term strategy. The problem is that people will like you at first, but once they realize work isn't getting completed, they start liking you less and less. They realize you aren't an effective leader who can help *them* grow.

That's what happened with Dominic, who allowed his peers and direct reports (at times) to make his decisions, sometimes even giving him direct orders in the process. They found that he was too accommodating and intuitively knew his approach was going to prevent their personal growth.

The first missing conversation I encouraged Dominic to have was an internal one. I asked him to reflect on the times when his people-pleasing strategy actually worked. He struggled to come up with examples. I asked him to think about what triggered his need to please, and we created a tool to help him stop his logic before it become problematic. As soon as he thought, *But what if they . . . ?* then he knew he was focused on people-pleasing rather than problem-solving and leading.

This process took several months, but he was eventually able to see the triggers more clearly when he could recognize his urge to agree with others, even when he didn't agree with their technical solutions. Then, he could rely on his technical expertise to push back much more professionally and with more useful solutions. He started to teach his team to diagnose issues the same way he did rather than agreeing with their (often inferior) analyses.

The second missing conversation was at the organizational level. I worked with both Dominic and his boss, the CEO, to get clearer on the communication norms and expectations in their company's culture. Did they prefer direct, candid, blunt, impersonal communication? Or did they want heightened-sensitivity communication, where they treated everyone like family members and tried not to hurt feelings—even at the expense of their business goals and individual performance?

Most culture should be a healthy, balanced combination of both, but very few companies take the time to talk about their communication norms and expectations. I've found that many companies going through rapid scaling from mom-and-pop headcounts (five to twenty five employees) to one hundred plus employees really struggle with developing effective internal communication norms around leadership communication behaviors. They don't know how to handle the necessary evil of adding bureaucracy to the culture—which feels impersonal (it is and should be)—but the goal is to universally apply rules equally across the board.

People don't like being rule enforcers, so they instead seek to please others. This disease is contagious and invasive, so removing it from your culture once you notice it is important for growing success.

Root Questions

- In what ways does your leadership team make decisions?
- How often do you self-censor your ideas when problem-solving with others?
- How does your team respond when one person goes against the accepted consensus of what others think?
- Can you think of people in your company who might exhibit the *disease to please*? How could you bring this up to them in a helpful manner?

Missing Conversation Quick Facts

CATEGORY	AVOIDANCE
Missing Conversation	Disease to Please
What It Does	When avoided, this rogue form of relationship building hides our true feelings and skills in favor of what we think is socially acceptable.
Why It Matters	Leads to too much reliance on consensus-based decision-making, creates errors, invites unnecessary risks, and crushes confidence.

CHAPTER 23

BRANDING IS IDENTITY

IT WAS A STRATEGIC ROLLUP SITUATION; THEY WERE growing in the Southeast region's long-term healthcare space and looking to acquire and consolidate several smaller competitors into its growing brand. Their stated goal was to streamline operations, cut costs, pool resources, and grow top-line revenue. Sun Health's plan made perfect sense in theory, but in practice it was proving much more difficult to execute for its ambitious CEO.

Carla was a twenty-five-year veteran of the long-term healthcare industry, having started an independent-living facility from scratch. Fundraiser, marketer, facilities manager, and impromptu line cook, Carla played every major role in her company over the years, eventually creating a "continuous care model" that included seamless transitions for her residents between independent living, assisted living, and 24/7 skilled care.

Carla recruited top-tier leaders from across the industry and set her sights on building a brand that attracted highly motivated team members and provided innovative, family-friendly services, medical support, social activities, and technologies for their residents. It was a concierge, white-glove-service long-term living facility, something very different from the 1980s nursing home model.

Fifteen years after opening her first facility, Carla had grown the brand to three different continuous care facilities and now wanted to "hypercharge" the growth through the rollup strategy. Within a two-year period, she acquired four other assets that had the space to expand from a single focus (independent living, assisted living, or 24/7 care) to the continuous care model. Because of the nature of the industry, many of these organizations operated as nonprofits, which allowed them to generate revenue from services, solicit donations, and reap the tax benefits, and Carla was leveraging this legal structure in her rollup strategy.

The first step of Sun Health's multi-site integration process was rebranding the new facilities under its branding guidelines. What Carla assumed would be a ninety-day project turned into a year-and-a-half-long struggle involving a range of challenges, including passionate arguments during meetings, subtle sabotage, a spike to double-digit voluntary attrition, and even a lawsuit. What Carla and her leadership team viewed as a simple step of altering the four logos to include Sun Health's colors, the organizational leadership teams (and their boards) at the newly acquired facilities viewed as a direct threat to their identities.

When organizations are being rebranded into a larger company's branding guidelines, we must understand that logos are part of organizational identity, and the people who work there—especially if they built that business from scratch—will be very attached to that symbol. If you want to minimize unproductive conflict and voluntary attrition of valuable team members, approach rebranding conversations with care and patience. If people are concerned that the changes will negatively impact the revenue mechanisms they have built (e.g., donor relationships), engage in thoughtful, open, and direct conversations about how those concerns will be addressed. For instance, being willing to sit down with the leadership team and core donors to ease concerns is a good step.

Altering logos and rebranding is simple from a technical point of view, but there are few things more personal to a businessperson who built a brand from scratch. The logo often cuts to the core of the business identity and the identities of the people who are behind that business.

Rebrand with care.

Root Questions

- What decisions might be unimportant, trivial, or small to you but could be very important to your team members?
- What organizational symbols evoke strong meanings for you and your team?
- When your team is experiencing change, do you build mechanisms to pulse-check the key goals and see the meanings that people are ascribing to them?

Missing Conversation Quick Facts

CATEGORY	AVOIDANCE
Missing Conversation	Branding and Identity
What It Does	Minimizes unproductive conflict and voluntary attrition of valuable team members by approaching rebranding conversations with diligence and patience.
Why It Matters	Altering logos and rebranding is simple from a technical perspective, but there are few things more personal to a business-person who built a brand from scratch.

CHAPTER 24

UNREALISTIC EXPECTATIONS

Brad couldn't believe that Andrew was termi-nated. He didn't know how to feel about his boss, mentor, and friend losing his job.

Andrew was the longest-serving senior director in his Fortune 500 health insurance company's history and also the highest paid individual at that level on the org chart. Andrew had worked in six different departments over his career, mastering the strategic revenue-generating side of the business, joint partnership development, and rebates and finance. He also showed talent for the intri-cate operational aspects of successfully leading project management teams across business functions. His ability to execute on cross-functional projects and implementa-tions involving billions of dollars was legendary within the company. Andrew knew the business model, helped build the company strategy, and found ways to continually create new revenue streams. He lived the company values and was a loyal team member.

But there was one thing Andrew couldn't control, and that was organizational politics. Because he had become such an asset to the company, more self-serving team members above Andrew on the org chart viewed him as a threat. Waves of terminations typically occur between twelve to eighteen months after a large company merger, after the press releases of job creation and synergistic efficiencies have faded from public headlines.

When Andrew texted Brad that he had been terminated, Brad was in a state of shock. He knew about organizational politics and was quite skilled at playing the game, but he didn't think his company would fire one of its most productive and knowledgeable team members. He was wrong.

Andrew told Brad to prepare himself, because the vice president that fired him would probably make Brad's job very difficult for the next six months. Luckily, Brad's team added a ton of value to the company, so Andrew didn't think Brad's job was on the chopping block, but he did advise Brad to double down on his influence game and to guard his communication with the vice president, whom Brad was now reporting to.

While Brad knew this was a bad move for his company, he also realized it was out of his control and that he had two choices: (a) put his head down, work hard, and produce results or (b) adopt a victim mentality, become a cynic, and quit. He chose to get to work and rallied his team to pull them out of their mental funk.

This started with his first meeting with the new vice president, where it was clear the VP had an extremely limited understanding of what Brad's team did or how they did it. Brad took the opportunity to catch his new boss up on the type of projects his team tackles, his team's stellar track record, and how his team could take zombie projects off the VP's radar. More importantly, Brad asked a series of seemingly mundane questions to understand what makes the VP tick, what communication style the VP prefers, and the communication cadence the VP would like. These innocent and important questions laid a foundation of respect for the new relationship.

The VP knew that Brad was an A-player and let him know so in this conversation, of course, before saying that Brad's team would be taking on a lot more projects in the short term. This obvious "flatter and flatten" strategy didn't deter Brad. He brought up the idea of how important expectations are in successfully executing large projects, especially when they involve multiple business units and departments, and he said he wanted to understand and be 100 percent aligned with the VP's expectations. So, a few days later when the VP dumped an unrealistic amount of work onto Brad's desk—in addition to the ongoing projects his team was already managing—Brad brought back up the expectations conversation.

While he had a bit of anxiety in this conversation, he wasn't going to let his fear hold him back. He used his knowledge of the new VP's admitting that he is a "numbers person" to quantify the workload for each project, compared that to the total number of hours per week that Brad's team could work, and then recommended a prioritization road map to the new VP that demonstrated how they could tackle the projects in an order that made the most sense for corporate strategic initiatives.

The VP loved this approach, and they agreed upon a path forward. More importantly, Brad was able to successfully manage unrealistic expectations being thrust upon him and his team. And he did so from a collaborative perspective that built an ally in his new boss.

Instead of avoiding a challenging conversation, Brad used the knowledge of his new boss's work style and behavioral preferences to have a conversation that created alignment in a tough situation with limited trust.

Kings to you, Brad.

Root Questions

- How do you respond when political tactics and games appear in your company?
- How do you *wish* you would respond?
- In what ways do you build in ongoing opportunities to discuss expectations for projects, operations, and strategic initiatives?
- How do the team members' work-style preferences impact your planning and expectations for big projects?

Missing Conversation Quick Facts

CATEGORY	AVOIDANCE
Missing Conversation	Unrealistic Expectations
What It Does	Clarifies expectations and creates alignment and organizational health, preventing unnecessary inefficiencies from slowing down work.
Why It Matters	Organizational politics quickly emerge at the expense of driving results when unrealistic expectations are left undiscussed, which is never healthy for an organization.

SECTION 3

ADVERSITY

"You've got to go out on a limb sometimes because that's where the fruit is."

—WILL ROGERS

Many leaders recognize the importance of engaging in challenging conversations that can enhance their organization, but they often bypass these discussions due to adversity. This adversity stems from internal and external business risks, poor decision-making practices, crisis situations, tragedy, and change.

When leaders know key conversations should occur but allow adversity to derail and distract them, the result is various issues that often complicate, rather than simplify, the adversity. The question that leaders should be asking themselves is whether the juice is worth the squeeze.

CHAPTER 25

CALIBRATION CONVERSATIONS (PART 2)

I DISCUSSED EARLIER IN THE BOOK THAT LEADERS OFTEN neglect calibration conversations because they aren't aware they should be having them. At other times, people don't discuss these things because recalibrating a tool, process, structure, or goal is less important than another adversity we are already dealing with. It is a simple process of prioritization.

For instance, Charlie was a top salesmen in a large steel fabrication and manufacturing company who had been promoted to Director of Business Development. Part of his new role was managing the entire sales team. Revenue was down, and the sales team and company leaders thought the main cause was a specific new regulatory requirement and tariff that had hit their industry in the previous year—but sales were still slumping after they anticipated a rebound.

The company's traditional sales model was that each location was competing against the other locations for leads and sales conversions. But it was shifting to a more collaborative model where the units were expected to cooperate, and the incentive structure was altered to support this new system.

Even though he was now the leader of the sales team, Charlie was uncomfortable embracing the new company mandate of sales meetings that shared best practices, conducted start/stop/continue of key behaviors, and distributed market information. He told me he wouldn't have liked this when he was a sales rep, because it would have hurt his commissions. Charlie felt the market slump, and the new information-sharing expectation was too much adversity. His confidence was negatively impacted, and his team was picking up on it.

Charlie was approaching the implementation of the new standard from a scarcity mindset, thinking that sharing this information would hurt his team's ability to hit their sales quotas. In addition, he had not fully accepted the new reality, that this was happening whether he wanted it to or not. The sales model had been recalibrated, but he wasn't willing to fully commit to it because he had no say in the new approach and because he felt it would negatively impact his job. He was guided by fear but unable to articulate what he was thinking.

Through our coaching, it became clear he felt the market trouble might lead to the company closing its doors. If the company didn't go out of business, he was also concerned with losing status, commissions, and potentially his job. Adversity stings. And the pain hurts even worse when, instead of treating the wound, we pour salt in it with negative thinking and inaction.

Charlie and I grabbed an in-person conversation with his boss (the CEO) about his concerns, especially because it was becoming apparent to Charlie's peers that the sales team was not embracing the new "team-based approach" to sales. We had an excellent candid and productive conversation, and his boss was able to ease most of his concerns and share concrete examples of how his peers were benefitting from the new information-sharing approach and maintaining (at least) current commission levels. In addition, I encouraged the CEO to share company financials[40] with Charlie to demonstrate that the company had a strong balance sheet. That put Charlie's mind at ease and helped him more readily embrace the new sales structure.

The CEO was so impressed with Charlie's change that he decided to implement a more transparent financial culture to share relevant company financial information with all managers and directors.

Just because adversity exists doesn't mean you have to embrace a lack of accountability. Conduct calibration conversations to reorient yourself and your team to high standards. These conversations create the *bamboo barriers* that will help your company grow in the direction you desire rather than in an unpredictable manner fertilized with fear.

Root Questions

- What conversations are deprioritized when revenue is down? Make a list.
- How do you get people to accept and adopt the new behaviors and expectations when your organization rolls out a new internal program?
- What role does the leadership team have in the previous question?
- What key ideas, standards, programs, and expectations need to be revisited on a quarterly basis to ensure they are still taking the company in the right direction?[41]

Missing Conversation Quick Facts

CATEGORY	ADVERSITY
Missing Conversation	Calibration Conversations
What It Does	Alleviates team members' tendency to deprioritize recalibrating a tool, process, structure, or goal when they are dealing with adversity.
Why It Matters	Not calibrating an issue to ensure it is heading in the right direction can amplify adversity and lead to even less accountability.

CHAPTER 26

ACCOUNTABILITY WITHOUT AUTHORITY

ONE OF THE MOST CHALLENGING TOPICS MY COACHING partners bring up is the idea of leading, managing, and influencing peers. Dealing with direct reports gets easier with time, but it takes a nimble mind and a full toolbox of communication skills and styles to effectively lead peers.

The hardest aspect of peer leadership is helping them stay committed to long-term projects that must drive visible results for the organization. Being awarded control of a project or initiative is exciting but comes with additional responsibilities and new things to learn, and this type of adversity (i.e., new responsibility) usually takes center stage as the project kicks off. This whole process becomes even more challenging for younger leaders who lack experience and people-development skills. Peer leadership is equally difficult for executive leaders who don't prioritize people development and communication.

Comparatively speaking, it's less complicated to lead people who directly report to you, because you can give directives they can usually carry out as long as you are clear and consistent in your messaging, and of course, if what you are discussing is tied to their role and responsibility. What becomes much more challenging is trying to get things done with people you do not have direct authority over. How do you help them be accountable to a project you're both working on?

Rebecca is an all-star nonprofit leader with natural people-development skills, not to mention being a high-character human being. Many high-performing leaders at the top of their game seek out experts to give them a little more of an edge, always sharpening their saw, which is how Rebecca and I formed a coaching partnership. She wanted to improve her ability to navigate difficult conversations, so we were working on a variety of specific behaviors related to that theme, such as helping her exert more assertiveness with peers when she lacked clear authority.

We had to get very specific with the types of people she was dealing with, what motivated them, their typical behavioral patterns, and her workplace relationship history with them. We developed a list of the most important missing conversations, including plainspoken clarity on project goals, how to divide and conquer goal completion, and defining what accountability without authority sounded like as the project unfolded. She even brought the phrase "accountability without authority" into conversations with her peers, and they appreciated her candor and directness.

Being transparent with what *accountable communication* sounds like is extremely important because it lays the expectations and framework for mutual respect. It also serves as an anchor all parties can use to reorient themselves when things get choppy. When the "accountability without authority" conversation is missing, silence and eggshell environments usually take its place. And then, missed goals and failed projects eventually show up, leading to even more adversity.

I encouraged Rebecca to use a simple three-step prompt for this conversation:

1. From my perspective, we are working on a project for which neither of us has full authority, and we are both concerned with creating excellent results.

2. My main goal is to make sure we talk through project details and decision-making expectations to make sure we stay *aligned* throughout the project.

3. Do you agree, and are you open to that conversation?

The essence of this discussion is to clearly point out that neither party has direct authority over one another, to find ways to manage the project while honoring each other's expertise, and to ensure project success. Having a kickoff conversation around project strategy, tactics, resource allocation, oversight, and management styles is a must-needed starting place. This deceptively simple approach keeps unhealthy organizational politics in check and turns a one-sided monologue into a true two-party dialogue. More successful results emerge when people recognize they are *accountable to each other* and *responsible for the tasks, timeline, and results.*[42]

The details around this conversation are also important, such as having it in a clear but informal manner, when both parties have time to focus. I suggest doing so in private rather than in front of the rest of the team, as this allows people to remove professional masks and be more authentic with each other. Rebecca used this three-step prompt so successfully on a variety of cross-functional projects that she now trains her direct reports to use the same process.

Root Questions

- How often do you expect your team members to exert accountability without authority with their peers?
- How do you manage this type of adversity?
- What are other ways to apply the three-step prompt within your organization?
- Do you agree with the idea that we are *accountable* to people and *responsible* for things? Why or why not?

Missing Conversation Quick Facts

CATEGORY	ADVERSITY
Missing Conversation	Accountability Without Authority
What It Does	Lays out the expectations and framework for mutual respect and serves as an anchor all parties can use to reorient themselves when things get choppy on a project.
Why It Matters	When the "accountability without authority" conversation is missing, silence and eggshell environments usually take its place, which are quickly filled with missed goals and failed projects, leading to even more adversity.

CHAPTER 27

CATEGORICAL IMPERATIVE

L ET'S TALK PHILOSOPHY.

Philosophy should not be an intimidating term—it is a framework of knowledge or principles that can guide decisions. But there is a big difference between *thinking* philosophically and *acting* philosophically. Few philosophers run successful businesses for a reason, and yet, it is extremely important to understand the principles that underlie our actions and decisions. A philosophical (principle-driven) approach can help us change them when they no longer serve us.

The categorical imperative is a conceptual tool advocated by one of the world's most famous philosophers, Immanuel Kant.[43] To put it simply, the categorical imperative approach encourages people to ask themselves, "Would it be right if everyone did this?" It helps us think about our actions by hypothetically turning them into a universal rule that everyone must follow and what the implications of that would be.

Would it be right if everyone did this? is a powerful question and reflective exercise that leaders should think through daily. It forces you to hold a mirror up to your mindset, your problem-solving style, your communication preferences, and your conflict-management norms.

Would your organization be more productive or less productive if categorically, everyone had to act the same way you do? There is no easy answer to this question, but it does lead to adversity identification. Because there are certain behaviors and thought patterns leaders would advocate that are clearly useful to an organization, but there are others that would create barriers and bottlenecks.

The goal is first to separate our workplace behaviors into two groups: productive and unproductive. Then, to strive to reduce or eliminate the unproductive behaviors over time and amplify the productive ones.

Thinking through the categorical imperative as applied to your workplace behaviors might uncover adversity that prevents us from taking positive action. It also might uncover adversity that we *create* through our actions, like having a challenging conversation but doing so at the wrong time, with the wrong tone, or in front of the wrong audience. Remember that communication usually escalates or de-escalates a volatile issue, so haphazard communication in delicate situations—where we exhibit a *Ready-Fire-Aim* mentality—adds to adversity.

If your behaviors became the "category" or expectation for how everyone thought and acted, would it lead to more or less empathy and connection in your company? More or less innovation? More or less productivity? This activity heightens our behavioral self-awareness and reminds us that we want productive behaviors to grow aboveground in a way that we can influence. We should not want to contribute to a set of behaviors that is always out of sight, out of mind, like a hidden and untended nest of bamboo roots, waiting to shoot up in unplanned areas. The absence of a reflective activity like the categorical imperative can accelerate the dulling of our awareness and the forgetfulness of what was once important.

The answers matter less than the exercise, of drawing your attention to the potent and subtle power of your communication patterns and how the way we communicate can create adversity or eliminate it.

Root Questions

- What are the most important principles that guide your actions in the workplace?
- What behavior *creates* the most adversity for your organization?
- What behavior *removes* the most adversity for your organization?

Missing Conversation Quick Facts

CATEGORY	ADVERSITY
Missing Conversation	Categorical Imperative (Universal Rule)
What It Does	Encourages people to ask themselves, "Would it be right if everyone did this?" serving as a reflective tool to understand the implications of our actions.
Why It Matters	Forces you to hold a mirror up to your mindset, your problem-solving style, your communication preferences, and your conflict-management norms and hopefully make adjustments as needed.

CHAPTER 28

CUSTOMER DIS-SERVICE

I HAVE WORKED WITH A LOCAL PHYSICAL THERAPIST ON a variety of injuries over the last few years. I liked the therapist's approach and loved that they were located within walking distance of my home. I recently switched physical therapists, however, not because of anything the therapist did but because of how I was treated by his receptionist, who is also his brother.

I arrived for an appointment at 2:00 p.m., and the receptionist informed me that they had me down for a 2:30 p.m. appointment. I thought that was odd, because I always confirm appointments when I set them, as "schedule Tetris" is a huge part of my job as a consultant and coach. I'm constantly having to shuffle meetings because of dynamic client calendars.

I let the receptionist know that unfortunately I was unable to make that work because of an upcoming business call and said that I would just reschedule after I returned from a vacation I was leaving for the next day. He said, "No problem," and wished me a good day.

He called me about an hour later, and my intuition predicted the reason before I ever answered the call. I was right.

After getting me on the line, his first statement was, "You are going to find this petty, but we have to charge you a rescheduling fee."

I knew their policy was to charge $25 for rescheduling appointments, so I told him it was fine to charge me the $25—even though I *did* show up for the appointment. It was annoying, but again, I liked my physical therapist and figured $25 wasn't worth throwing a wrench in the relationship.

"Actually, because you rescheduled less than twenty-four hours before your appointment, we have to charge you $60—the full price of the session you would have had."

That was too far. My patience meter was out of quarters, and Dr. Furey[44] wasn't around to help me break a dollar. I brusquely told the receptionist to charge me the fee and then do what was necessary to close my account, as I would be finding another physical therapist.

You would have thought this man was struck by lightning; he was in awe of this "voting with your dollars" approach to business. He began to argue with my decision, which I found amusing, telling me why this was a bad idea, that they had a reasonable policy, and that he couldn't do anything about the policy (which wasn't true, as he and his brother ran the business). His defensiveness was a clear indication that at some level, he realized he was making a choice to provide poor customer service.

He continued to lecture me on the phone for three minutes. As a sidenote, this person did not understand the economic concept of *opportunity cost.* Just using back-of-the-napkin math, I can say pretty confidently that his office had profited more than $2,000 after taxes from me over the last few years and was set to profit at least $600 more from upcoming appointments. Plus, I had referred two clients to their business over the last year.

If this call had been "recorded for quality training purposes," you would have thought the policy the receptionist was being forced to follow was one of the Ten Commandments. He spoke of the cancellation fee with such reverence, and his flabbergasted tone indicated he had no understanding that all policy is a *choice,* an organizational *decision tool* that can be adapted and flexed based on reasonable need. This was lost on him.

Maybe he really didn't have authority to make the exception, but that didn't feel like the case on our call. It felt more like ego, like he'd challenged me to a game of chicken and then couldn't believe I didn't cave in to his pressure.

This business adversity was created due to a missing conversation. It could have gone like this:

"Hi, Mr. Schaefer, I'm going to do you a $60 favor. We actually have a twenty-four-hour last-minute rescheduling policy that I'm sure you weren't aware of, but because you've been a long-term and valued client, we are going to waive that $60 for you today. Just please reschedule any appointments at least twenty-four hours in advance in the future so you don't get hit with that fee!"

Policies are useful... until they aren't.

Policies are choices that organizations make to solve patterned problems with the goal of making work more efficient and effective. But things regularly pop up that don't fit that pre-patterned mold. Be sure your team members know how and when to adapt them to unique situations with customers. This is how you prevent perhaps the deadliest form of adversity for any organization: customer dis-service.

Root Questions

- How important is customer service at your organization?
- What constitutes the categories of high-quality, acceptable, and unacceptable customer service?
- What role do policies and procedures play in delivering consistent, high-quality customer service?
- Do you train your people on *discretion boundaries*, teaching the art of when/how to bend a rule to please a customer and when not to? If so, how? If not, how could you start?

Missing Conversation Quick Facts

CATEGORY	ADVERSITY
Missing Conversation	Customer Dis-service by Ignoring Discretion
What It Does	Makes sure your team members know how and when to adapt a policy to unique situations with customers.
Why It Matters	Policies are choices that organizations make to solve patterned problems with the goal of making work more efficient and effective, but situations arise that don't fit the mold, and when people don't know what to do they will create more adversity.

CHAPTER 29

CHANGE AND FEEDBACK

CHANGE AND FEEDBACK MUST BE KEPT IN LOCKSTEP with one another. They are the peanut butter and jelly of moving your company from A to B.

While Julius intuitively understood the importance of providing feedback to others during his company's change process, he did not have a handle on how to effectively do so in a helpful way, and his self-awareness of his communication skills was low. So, the day-to-day actions of doubling the physical footprint and headcount of the marketing company he'd founded ten years earlier were much bumpier than they should have been. The following scenario led Julius to retain me as a coach and work on the additional adversity that emerged because of his change-management communication decisions and behaviors.

Throughout the change process, instead of delegating and empowering others to lean into responsibility, he micromanaged processes and projects, spending hours each day pouring over project management software, sending reminder emails and texts, and questioning his team members' decision-making. These "in-the-weeds" actions robbed Julius of essential time and energy that he should have been spending on capital expenditure (CapEx) decisions, balance sheet management, retaining his talented team, and clarifying his company's vision during this challenging time. Instead, his need for control over easily quantifiable tasks and his fear to wade into the deep end of uncertainty turned him into a different person.

Micromanagement is the canary in the coal mine, as it can only mean a few things: (a) an individual needs coaching to enhance self-awareness, better prioritize their actions, learn to delegate, and monitor their need for control; (b) the company is operating a poorly defined system; or (c) both of these things.

When two of Julius's leadership team members brought the implications of his constant micromanaging during change to his attention—finally finding the courage to share with him the demoralization that was spreading through the organization—he fired one of them (two weeks later) and blamed the cultural issues on that individual. The other team member left three weeks after her peer was terminated. Top talent walks when they realize their growth and their voice are not priorities. Julius learned that the hard way. His lack of self-awareness was amplified during the adversity of organizational change. Our coaching kicked off in the aftermath of this invasive chaos.

If you can't handle feedback, you won't survive change.

And if you don't provide consistent and clear feedback while leading change in your organization, your employees won't survive change.

Employees are hound dogs at sniffing out the mismatch between consistent actions and espoused values, so when actions and values are misaligned, distrust and pessimism run rampant. When your company is engaging in a high-stakes, long-term change process, you must establish a cadence of updates and feedback that runs both directions. If you don't, the only feedback you will receive are the reasons people quit when having their exit interviews with HR.

Root Questions

- What does micromanaging mean to you?
- How does organizational change impact your communication behaviors?
- What does rampant micromanaging say about your company's mission, vision, values, and strategy?

Missing Conversation Quick Facts

CATEGORY	ADVERSITY
Missing Conversation	Change and Feedback
What It Does	Providing constructive feedback leads to a more distributed and shared workload. Clear guidance also reduces the need for micromanagement, allowing more efficiency and growth to emerge.
Why It Matters	During poorly communicated change, micromanaging often becomes the primary organizational force, thereby limiting organizational effectiveness and results, and minimizing individuals' skill growth and engagement.

CHAPTER 30

CONFLICT IS FERTILIZER

I ASK PEOPLE ALL THE TIME WHAT CONFLICT MEANS TO them, and less than 10 percent of my audience members at speaking engagements, coaching clients, and workshop participants have positive connotations about that term. They usually frame it as a negative experience, something unpleasant, something to be avoided, something to be contained. Yelling. Arguing. Digging in. Difficult personalities. These are common phrases they associate with conflict.

It is rare for a leader to think about conflict's hidden quality: its ability to grow relationships and companies.

At its core, conflict means disagreement. Think of any healthy personal or professional relationship that lacks disagreement, and I'll show you decay and atrophy. When appropriately structured, conflict is fertilizer; things grow *because* of it, not *in spite* of it. It might be dirty and stinky, and few people want to be knee-deep in it all day—much like manure-based fertilizer in gardening—but well-structured conflict and effective confrontation produce miraculous growth for ideas and innovation.

Conflict is often thought of as a form of adversity, but it doesn't have to be. That is a choice.

Creating and implementing a framework and expectations to manage big disagreements in the workplace is much easier than randomly reacting to them as they emerge. The key is baking the framework—and a physical space—into the daily operations of your business.

Where we disagree in the workplace is almost as important as *how* we disagree. Giving the process and space a name that aligns with the company's culture will go a long way to embracing the reality that disagreement is an acceptable part of successful organizations and demonstrate that you "do disagreement" a certain way at your organization.

The Laundry Room, The War Room, The Arena, The Pool—these are a few names that my clients have created for their disagreement process to challenge, engage, and build ideas together. The process should be simple and should reinforce mutual respect and honesty, with a reminder that the goal of a spirited discussion is idea generation, accuracy, and growth.

Here's a common set of guidelines for well-structured conflict and effective confrontation. Feel free to do some R&D—"rip off and duplicate"—to make them your own:

1. Ideas that drive results. The purpose of spirited discussion is good ideas, understanding, and alignment that helps the company. It's not necessarily about agreement.

2. Use the right space for high-emotion disagreements.

3. Seek to understand first, then to be understood.
4. When in doubt, ask questions.
5. Monitor your tone. When emotions are flaring, *how* you say something is as important as *what* you say.

With over fifteen hundred hours of domestic and employment mediation experience, I know firsthand that the worst thing humans can do with high-emotion disagreements is ignore them, acting like they don't exist or that they will solve themselves. Not only will topics like child custody (personal life) or splitting liabilities and equity (professional life) not work themselves out on their own, but major disagreements left undiscussed get worse over time, never better. The issues grow underground resentments hidden from the light of day, and these additional adversities eventually sprout up and decrease the identification of common ground between people.

Don't make conflict a bigger problem than it really is. It's just a disagreement, so manage it with the same strategic mindset that you would your balance sheet, project management software, or hiring process decisions.

Root Questions

- How well does your organization handle workplace conflict?
- What is your personal response when conflict emerges in the workplace? What is the company expectation?
- How does your communication change during workplace conflict?
- How *should* your communication change during workplace conflict?
- What frameworks, processes, or expectations do you and/or your organization have in place for how people should deal with conflict?

Missing Conversation Quick Facts

CATEGORY	ADVERSITY
Missing Conversation	Conflict Is Fertilizer
What It Does	Conflict is disagreement, and when it is appropriately structured, conflict acts as fertilizer. Things grow *because* of it, not *in spite* of it.
Why It Matters	Creating and implementing a framework and expectations to manage high-stakes workplace disagreements is easier than randomly reacting to them as they emerge; the key is baking the framework into the daily operations of your business.

CHAPTER 31

GROUP GRIEVING

A S A PROFESSIONAL SPEAKER, I GET THE PRIVILEGE AND
pleasure of speaking to business owners, leaders,
founders, and top-tier managers around the world. One of
my favorites is an organization called Vistage, the largest
CEO peer-coaching group in the world. This is a special
group of business leaders, because they have chosen to
invest in themselves and learn through peer coaching and
from subject matter experts.

One of the most unique Vistage presentations I ever
gave had less to do with the content and more to do with
the kickoff. A CEO in this group had recently lost her adult
child in a tragic accident, and this in-person group meeting
was the first time she was connecting with her Vistage
group since then.

The group, of course, wanted to respect the wishes
of this individual, so the original plan was to just treat
the session like any other group meeting. Luckily, the
chair of this Vistage group is an extremely professional

communicator and veteran Vistage chair, a person who exhibits best practices in everything he does professionally. More important, he embodies the Vistage mission of helping CEOs live their best lives.

In talking with the chair, we wanted to respect his member's wishes by not making the situation the focus of the day, but it was important to allow for some momentary group grieving, as there would have been a lot of unexpressed emotion, anxiety, and tension in the room. This was clear from other members who arrived early and were visibly affected and explicitly stated they wanted to offer comforting thoughts to their peer and friend.

The chair and I felt it best for me to leave the room since I did not have a personal relationship with his member, and it would be more appropriate for the group to have emotionally difficult but important conversations without a third-party observer around.

The group chair shared the three-step strategy we came up with on the fly and got their buy-in: Air, Dig, Reflect. First, they would have a thirty-minute conversation to air the emotions and let other group members express their support and concern for this individual. Next, I would facilitate an engaging discussion. Finally, the group would end their day with reflective thoughts and conversations, helping them to continue the group-grieving process.

This was a first for me as a professional speaker, and I was more nervous[45] than usual, as I have never had to "perform" what is typically an energetic, engaging, and humorous presentation after a tone-shift in the opposite direction. Of course, this was nothing compared to what the member was feeling.

Upon entering the room, my strategy was simple. I extended my heartfelt sympathy directly to the member and then asked that person and the group if I had their permission to go about my presentation in my normal manner, providing disclaimers about what they could expect from my style (i.e., humor, some cursing, real-world examples, candidness). Not only did the group agree, but they also visibly breathed a sigh of relief and were able to thoroughly engage our discussion. I used a crescendo tactic to my energy and volume to ease into my natural style, opting not to kick off with my immediate high-energy, in-your-face approach. The discussion turned out as well as it could have.

Part of me wanted to run away from this adversity, to reschedule the presentation. I mean, how can a high-energy, fun-filled professional speaker be expected to perform in such a difficult circumstance?

And then it hit me just how selfish that thought was, just how minuscule my challenge was compared to what that member was experiencing. I reframed my attitude while waiting during their discussion and made it my sole goal to help the group apply the purpose of that day's presentation: Understanding others is the fastest way to build strong relationships.

Their group practiced that same principle prior to our discussion. That was a proud moment for me and a lesson I shared later that day with my kids.

Root Questions

- How does your organization handle grieving in the workplace?
- What is your normal response when tragedy strikes that affects the workplace?
- How does your communication change during tragedy that affects the workplace?
- How *should* your communication change during tragedy that affects the workplace?
- What can you do differently to honor your team members and employees going through tragedy while also maintaining business operations?

Missing Conversation Quick Facts

CATEGORY	ADVERSITY
Missing Conversation	Group Grieving
What It Does	Allows unexpressed emotions, anxiety, and tensions to be discussed out in the open in as straightforward a manner as possible when dealing with tragedy.
Why It Matters	If the emotions and anxieties stay bottled up at a group level, they will eventually explode out in an unhealthy manner, as this elephant (tragedy as adversity) creates more adversity from being ignored.

CHAPTER 32

THE AMBUSH

THE TWO MEN JUMPED UP FROM THEIR DESKS AND rushed toward each other, bouncing chests and shouting obscenities. The other office workers held their breath, and some looked down at the paperwork on their desks. The tension and anger were immense, and no one knew what to do.

My coaching client was finishing a call in a different area of the building when his colleague burst through his door and said, "Your guys are about to kill each other! You should probably do something."

My client's company was a third-generation, family-owned plumbing supply and distribution firm, built from the bootstraps. Many of the managers used abrasiveness, fear, and volume as their main tools to get things done. This was just how things worked there. It was how they'd always done it.

Loyalty was what mattered and what was rewarded—but my client wanted to do things differently. He wanted to expand his communication tool belt and connect with and motivate others without having to first jump to fear-based management tactics.

His COO liked this approach and hired me to coach Derek, their lead estimator and project manager, in how to effectively delegate, remain assertive, ensure accountability, and drive results. Most importantly, Derek had to learn to let go of small tasks and surrender his perfectionism.

Upon entering the scene of the shouting, Derek pulled the guys apart and talked to them separately. He was able to help calm each of them down, and everyone else got back to business quickly. While the immediate threat had passed, Derek knew he had a problem on his hands, so he called me once he got some private time and asked to talk through the situation.

We discussed how each person possessed strengths and weaknesses, and Derek wasn't sure if he should immediately terminate the person who caused the issue or not. The problem was, they couldn't afford to terminate either worker, because they needed them both to help the company catch up on a backlog of work.

Apparently, the entire episode had unfolded because a line item was entered on the wrong spot on an estimation form, but instead of pointing this out to a colleague, one of the men involved in the scuffle took a more...Machiavellian approach.

This mischievous individual walked over to the desk of the man who made the error, picked up that man's phone, dialed a number, and put the call on speakerphone— with several coworkers within earshot. When someone answered the call, the man who dialed the number said,

"Tell him what you did." It turns out he had called a supervisor and was trying to get the man who made the error in trouble and to look bad in front of his peers while doing so.

The supervisor on the other end of the line had no clue what was going on, and the instigator's coworker didn't even know who was now speaking through his own desk speakerphone.

"You screwed up the estimation form," the gruff employee said to his now-incensed colleague. "You're going to cost us all a lot of money. Great job."

Truly, this was the work of a master communicator.

Once on the scene, Derek handled it beautifully, both in the moment to de-escalate things and in the aftermath to lay out the action plan. Instead of letting people cool off and then getting back to work, as some of his colleagues suggested, he took the difficult route.

He held the missing conversation.

Derek talked with Human Resources and walked HR through his plan, which involved formal write-ups for each individual, as well as performance-improvement plans with clear course-of-action clauses if certain behaviors occurred or results were not achieved. Derek then talked to each person individually to explain the plan, and then convened all three of them together to have the coworkers talk directly to each other. This, of course, uncovered a variety of issues that had led to the blowup.

Derek's HR department was extremely impressed with how he handled himself, and while it doesn't guarantee the guys won't get into it again, they were given crystal clarity on how they will all proceed if they do. Derek set everyone up for success, clarified and reinforced his company's professionalism standards, and treated his direct reports with respect—especially considering he had ample justification for their immediate terminations.

Root Questions

- What do you do when anger (or physical confrontation) emerges in the workplace?
- In what ways do you coach your people to properly de-escalate intense disagreements?
- Is your organizational culture one in which multiple people would try to positively intervene in an issue like this, or one where people would cower from a chance to be helpful?
- How might you have handled this situation? What would you have done differently?

Missing Conversation Quick Facts

CATEGORY	ADVERSITY
Missing Conversation	The Ambush
What It Does	De-escalating high-stress, high-emotion disagreements addresses the immediate adversity in the room rather than letting it linger, but defusing the situation with urgency should only be the first step in a two-step process.
Why It Matters	Ignoring the second step of de-escalation by not discussing what led to the original blowup (after people cool down) guarantees the blowup will recur.

CHAPTER 33

GENERATIVE PEOPLE

THERE ARE LEADERS IN THE WORKPLACE WHO EXUDE confidence, positivity, and productivity. Their demeanor is pleasant and results are plentiful. We can label these special beings as *generative people*, and we should try to employ as many of them as possible. They generate goodwill, good solutions, and good times wherever they go. We should all strive to be these people and fill our teams and companies with them, and if we are lucky enough, even marry one.[46]

But there is another type of generative people, except the things they generate don't add to the success and value of a company; they take away from it.

These people generate feelings of despair and confusion. They seek allies in their misery and have a natural talent for victimizing and playing the martyr. Things always seem to happen to them; they rarely have agency to take action or steer the ship in a different direction.

Psychologists call this having an *external locus of control*, which I argue is the dark side of creativity and productivity. These individuals are *creating* a climate of distrust. They are *producing* a culture where excuses are normalized, accountability is gaslighted, and benchmarks are questioned. These people generate an atmosphere that prevents innovation and leads to value destruction because it forces others to deal with their negativity and pessimism.[47]

With a wave of their whine, these negatively generative team members can derail a useful meeting or prevent a constructive conversation. Leaving a trail of adversity in their wake seems to be their superpower.

Positively generative people have the opposite effect and can often (though not always) counteract the effects of negativity through their valuable and impactful insights. A positively generative leader's communication package—their approach, eye contact, posture, facial expressions, tone, timing, volume, word selection—seems to be the antidote to the fog of confusion that quickly overwhelms teams. And this battle between negative and positive generators is amplified during times of organizational change or crisis, when every action, decision, goal, and process is interpreted through a lens of anxiety and insecurity. The positively generative people resemble a manicured grove of bamboo that others stop to admire, while negatively generative people are more like a jungle of bamboo that people strive to avoid.

Great leaders and positively generative people do not allow their team members to drive BMWs: bitching, moaning, whining. These are the forms of negativity that spread like wildfire and catch the underbrush of uncertainty ablaze.

Strive instead to be a positively generative person, raising others' ambitions and initiating aspirational thinking.[48] What is more valuable to your company? Spending time to unwind the havoc caused by negatively generative people or having the conversations up front that prevent the acceptance of these behaviors in the first place?

Root Questions

- How do you respond to negativity (complaining, whining) in the workplace?
- How do you draw the line between unproductive complaining and healthy venting?
- How might you advise younger managers how to spot the difference in the above question?
- Make a list of positively generative people in your workplace. What are you doing to keep them engaged and positively challenged?
- Make a list of negatively generative people in your workplace. What are you doing to increase their awareness of this behavior and help them eliminate it?

Missing Conversation Quick Facts

CATEGORY	ADVERSITY
Missing Conversation	Generative People
What It Does	Talking through what we generate through our communication behaviors and whether our behaviors create or remove adversity form the workplace is a productive activity.
Why It Matters	A positively generative person raises others' ambitions and initiates aspirational thinking, whereas a negatively generative person creates a climate of distrust, normalizes excuses, and gaslights accountability.

CHAPTER 34

SURPRISE ATTACKS

O NE OF MY COACHING CLIENTS, DEBBIE, WAS HAVING AN issue with a team member that was not one of her direct reports.

Debbie had fiduciary responsibility of the civil engineering division in a large construction company. The P&L was her responsibility, and this included any cross-functional projects that ended up as line items on her financial statements.

The entire enterprise was in the process of modernizing its support systems and updating technology stacks through the digitization of all standard operating procedures and workflows. This made sense in theory, but in practice it was an extremely challenging change project, especially when changes touched multiple departments and functions. Interdepartmental changes can make it unclear who has formal authority over the process change, and this particular company came from a traditional culture that is abrasive to change in the first place.

The change project was unfolding without many major issues, but then a nagging concern hit Debbie's desk. The team in the shipyards was pushing back hard against the digitization process, instead embracing their traditional paper-and-pencil approach to scheduling, accounts receivable/payable, and inventory management. This was causing second-order effects for shipments coming in and out of the shipyard, which was going to negatively impact the P&L, in addition to causing bad blood and decreased trust between departments. Her employee asked if she would get involved in the messaging to motivate the shipyard team to get behind the changes, and she did, but her emails fell on blind eyes.

She brought the issue to the attention of the Shipyard Director, even though it was outside of her authority domain. The yard workers not falling in line with the change all reported to the director, a longtime organizational member who was well-respected and considered an old-school, loyal company man. It's not that Debbie had a *bad* relationship with this person; she just didn't have much of one at all. He seemed receptive to getting the issue addressed when they spoke briefly on the phone, so she was encouraged when she received an email to have a meeting in his office about it.

When she showed up to his office, the director was present, as were several members from the shipyard department. As Debbie walked through the door, the director teed off the conversation with, "So, what's the problem you've got with my team?"

He did not deliver his question in a playful or ironic way; it was an aggressive and defensive posture. No smile, all teeth.

The next ten minutes were unproductive, abrasive, and didn't solve anything, as Debbie realized this was a losing battle to argue her position in this setting. She called me immediately after the meeting and briefly vented, and then I asked a lot of questions. From there, we strategized for a *Respectful Reset (RR)*.

The Respectful Reset is when a leader recognizes that a conversation is going very poorly—which can arise for many different reasons—and, instead of addressing it in the moment with a variety of stakeholders in the room, opts for a private conversation. This helps people save face and respects their authority. The RR is also useful when a relationship has a problematic history, a pattern of poor communication, lack of trust, or blatant dislike for one another. An RR involves a few simple steps:

1. *Setting*: Conduct the one-on-one discussion in a private, neutral setting—if possible, outside of either person's office. The best setting is a "walk and talk."

2. *The Reset*: Explicitly ask for a "reset" in the situation or relationship, acknowledging your observation that things are not as effective as they could be.

3. *Seek Understanding*: Seek to understand the other person's position first. Ask questions.

4. *Your Perspective*: Only present your perspective after you fully understand theirs.

5. *Voltron Value*: Ask if they are willing to combine ideas to build a better solution with you that creates value for all parties.

Debbie followed this process and was not only able to move the digitization project forward with only limited (and manageable) speed bumps in the shipyard, but she also vastly improved her relationship with the well-respected director, where they continued to crowdsource ideas to innovate for the company.

He later confessed that he appreciated her direct approach with him and knew that he can come off as intimidating, even saying that he could have handled the situation better by not surprising her with that meeting.

Lean into adversity to turn it into an advantage.

Root Questions

- Who in your organization might you need to reset with?
- In what ways does your company turn adversity/ disadvantages into advantages?
- Who has an intimidating presence in your organization, and is that style of presence useful for getting things done? Useful for who?
- How could you use the RR steps (or some of the steps) to positively impact culture at your organization?

Missing Conversation Quick Facts

CATEGORY	ADVERSITY
Missing Conversation	Surprise Attacks and The Reset
What It Does	When we get verbally attacked in the workplace, we can choose to let it lie or we can choose to work through the adversity using the *Respectful Reset*.
Why It Matters	Helps people save face, respects others' authority, and digs into the topic to re-establish a productive working relationship.

CHAPTER 35

PARTNER BUYOUT

CLAIRE AND TWO OF HER THREE BUSINESS PARTNERS agreed that Rita was no longer pulling her weight as a partner.

This challenging topic had been somewhat of a talking point at the manager meetings over the last eighteen months. It was a sensitive issue, as Claire and Rita had co-founded the company after working together at another firm. The duo brought on their other two partners sometime later. Despite being a co-founder, though, Rita was not doing business development at the same level or expectation as the other partners. She was also missing a lot of meetings by taking PTO and was not expanding current projects into future opportunities.

As an ownership team, all four partners had talked about this and were willing to get Rita a sales coach, but she continually recommitted and did a better job—for a while—and would then fall back into the pattern of working as an individual consultant and not as a company partner.

It was time for a change, because Claire and the other two partners were starting to have friction in areas they *thought* were unrelated to the Rita situation. They finally decided that they should buy out Rita, but they were unsure of the mechanics for how to do so.

Claire was one of my coaching partners and brought this to one of our meetings. I suggested they revisit their operating agreement, as there was most likely a partner buyout clause in it. There was, so she took that back to her two partners and they came up with a very fair buyout package, far beyond the minimum stipulations in their operating agreement.

The partners agreed that all three of them should deliver the message to Rita and that they were going to do so over a Zoom call. When Claire told me this, I didn't mince words, saying, "This is a terrible decision and disrespectful to the co-founder of your firm."

I asked, "Imagine you were presenting this situation to your daughter as a business case study to learn from. Could you make the case that this is the proper way to have this kind of conversation?"

She instantly said no and realized she had to deliver the message to Rita in a one-on-one conversation, but she still mentioned Zoom.

I asked, "Do you want Rita to be able to leave with as much dignity as possible? If so, do you truly believe a video chat would accomplish that?"

Without hesitation, Claire said she was booking a ticket to Georgia to deliver the news face-to-face. She flew down on a Friday morning and had a direct and unpleasant twenty-minute conversation with Rita. While emotionally challenging, the conversation didn't erupt into tears or anger, and then Claire flew back that same afternoon.

By the time Monday came around, Rita had reached out to Claire and thanked her, saying that she felt free and that she had lost the joy for the work a while ago, which was replaced by a feeling of self-loathing because she knew she wasn't pulling her partner weight. To this day—nearly six months after this scenario—Claire and Rita still have a great relationship, and Rita says she has never been happier, now that she's free to truly enjoy her retirement.

When having to terminate a close friend or business partner, conduct this conversation in person whenever possible. Equity, ownership, and buyout conversations are necessary (but not always sufficient) for creating the barriers that let teams get back to focusing on growth. It will rarely be a pleasant discussion, but it is the right thing to do.

Root Questions

- What might indicate that a key leader or business partner may no longer be effectively contributing to the team?
- How can these issues be addressed as early as possible?
- Why is it important to deliver high-impact but difficult news in person?
- What strategies and tactics can be employed to ensure that a high-impact, difficult conversation is conducted with respect and dignity?

Missing Conversation Quick Facts

CATEGORY	ADVERSITY
Missing Conversation	Partner Buyout
What It Does	Shines a light on a topic that touches every aspect of organizational life (business equity and ownership).
Why It Matters	If things change related to expected ownership behaviors, but this conversation is missing, adversity will emerge that could lead to the dissolution of the company.

CHAPTER 36

EMOTIONAL MUTE BUTTON

WHEN ADVERSITY STRIKES, A WHIRLWIND OF EMOTIONS usually strikes back. And when the epicenter of an emotional explosion is anger, it rarely leads to a quick and productive solution to a problem. It almost always creates more problems.

This is a common pattern for leaders who struggle with impatience, frustration, and anger. Counterintuitively, anger is a form of weakness, even though people believe it projects strength. As someone who constantly struggles with controlling his anger, frustration, and impatience, I know what I'm talking about.

When I let out my inner Hulk, it's because I feel like I can't control something or someone, and for whatever reason, my conditioned response is to lash out, tear down, and plow ahead. When unchecked, my Hulk communication style creates chaos, broken trust, and relationships in need of repair.

I've mentioned my psychologist, Dr. Furey, in several earlier chapters. I still work with him on an as-needed basis to assist with anger issues. Over the years, he has helped me reduce the frequency, duration, and intensity of my anger outbursts, and I have made a lot of progress—but I am by no means perfect. If I am not on guard, my anger will get the best of me. It's just who I am, but I don't let that behavioral trait (which is a flaw) trump my ability to improve myself.

Dr. Furey worked with me to figure out my "anger-escalation sequence." My anger flavor typically builds up over a period of time; I don't jump directly to full Hulk mode. If we could short-circuit the escalation sequence before I started seeing red, then Hulk would stay in the cage, and I wouldn't have to clean up a relational or organizational mess. Because for me, once I'm in full-on anger mode, there is no rational thinking or psychological tool that can bring me down. It just has to run its course . . . which is not pleasant for those around me.

My anger was never directed at my clients or coworkers but instead directed at those who love me most: my family. I used to often bring work stress into the home, adopt a victim mentality, and then let unimportant and petty annoyances build up to an anger explosion. Think crying over spilled milk. This was not fair to my family or myself.

Meeting regularly with Dr. Furey over an eighteen-month period early on, I put in the work to identify what triggered my anger sequences. They almost all started with a feeling of impatience that resulted from unnecessary busyness or situational urgency that someone was placing on me. I would feel like I was struggling in a mental straitjacket, the feeling of needing to get emerging tasks completed all at once.

Dr. Furey told me to carry a pack of LifeSavers, and when I started to feel impatient, I had to pop a candy in my mouth and not take action until that candy was gone. It was amazingly effective. And eventually I would chill out just by feeling the LifeSavers in my pocket.

I also got my wife and kids on board with keeping the Hulk caged, asking them to help me identify the early stages of this sequence, and they were happy to oblige. If you struggle with anger, learn your anger-escalation sequence and your anger triggers, and then use it as an emotional mute button to pause an upcoming negative explosion of energy. You can still release this energy; just do it in a more suitable and productive (or at least non-harmful) manner.

One of the best things you can do to avoid creating unnecessary adversity—either at work or in the home—is to find your emotional mute button and press it whenever anger arises. This gives you a healthier way to vent your frustration before the volume in your head gets too loud. Our emotions will always grow underground first, but learning how to apply an emotional mute button will prune them when they spring aboveground at unexpected times.

Root Questions

- What are common triggers that escalate your anger (or other common negative emotional responses)?
- What techniques or tools can you use to manage your anger (or other emotions) in the moment?
- How can involving your family, a trusted advisor, or colleagues in your emotional management process improve your relationships?
- What are healthier ways to release the energy from anger (or other emotions) without causing harm to yourself or others?

Missing Conversation Quick Facts

CATEGORY	ADVERSITY
Missing Conversation	Emotional Mute Button
What It Does	Being in touch with your most frequent and intensely expressed emotions allows you to direct them in a healthy manner and limit the adversity they can create.
Why It Matters	Even healthy emotions like joy can lead to unhealthy consequences when over-expressed in a workplace, so an increased emotional awareness gives you an additional tool.

CHAPTER 37

CONFLICT RADAR

I T'S SURPRISING HOW MANY CONFIDENT PEOPLE ARE secretly terrified of disagreement. Whether we call it confrontation, candid disagreement, or overt conflict, it is something that is part of every work environment. Having the ability to prepare for and navigate these scenarios is the mark of a seasoned communicator and one of the characteristics of leadership excellence. You cannot grow into an *elite* leader without mastering this skill: making conflict productive.

Scenarios that fall into the conflict conversations category might include:

- Arguing and negotiating a budget.
- Disagreeing over the timeline of a CapEx project with a vendor.
- Disagreeing over project-scope details.
- Sharing unpopular perspectives about team member performance.

The list is endless, but unfortunately so is people's creativity for avoiding or downplaying these important conflict conversations. As we learned a few chapters back, at its root conflict simply means disagreement.

I developed a tool to help my consulting clients and coaching partners build a sturdier foundation from which to engage in workplace disagreement. The Conflict RADAR serves the dual purpose of framework and metaphor to help leaders enhance their ability to deal with uncomfortable disagreement, remain calm despite stress, and turn a negative interaction into an organizational asset.

Because conflict is rife with fluid emotions and human psychology, there is no *formula* that can be universally applied to solve all disagreements amicably, but what follows is a set of *guidelines* that leaders can use to defuse uncomfortable situations.

Figure 6. The Conflict RADAR is a useful tool and metaphor.

R = Reflect: Pause before emotionally reacting to a situation, think it over

A = Analyze: Break down the situation into *who, what, where, when, why,* and *how*

D = Describe: Jot down the emotions/feelings that are being stirred up

A = Apply: Put together no more than five brief points that form your response plan

R = Respond: Engage in communication following the plan you built

The goal is to write out a brief plan following the acronym until this process becomes intuitive and notes are no longer necessary.[49] Based on the success of my coaching partners over the years, mastery of the Conflict RADAR takes between three and twelve months for vigilant leaders who use the tool consistently. From a minimal perspective, simply thinking about your Conflict RADAR is an essential first step.

How tightly calibrated is your RADAR? In other words, are you so sensitive that the smallest slight sets you off or makes you defensive? Are you triggered by everything? If that is the case, perhaps you need to adjust your RADAR's sensitivity setting. On the other extreme, perhaps your RADAR is calibrated so low that you lack any professionalism and are aloof to your communication style, how others are perceiving you, and the drama that bubbles up around you. Two examples will help us see the utility of the RADAR in action.

Gabrielle was the COO of a $165 million/year electrical contracting firm in the northeastern United States.

Her company was going through restructuring and was having to close several underperforming satellite offices. Turmoil, stress, uncertainty, and lawsuits were present, and she was charged with integrating the remaining team members into the restructured company. She used the Conflict RADAR to personally manage conversations with team members being terminated and with team members remaining on board. She took it a step further and baked the RADAR into their company culture, making it a tool to be included in their employee handbook and hung up in the back office. While it didn't make these conversations enjoyable, it helped make them effective, clear, and productive while simultaneously listening to people's concerns. Gabrielle was able to apply the Conflict RADAR as a tool on multiple levels to improve her own leadership communication behaviors and encourage those same behaviors in others through company culture.

Richard did not have such a good grasp of the Conflict RADAR. He is a third-generation owner in the wholesale grocery business who felt fear and loudness were more effective tools than connection and respect. When he took over as CEO, Richard's company had many long-tenured employees who had dedicated most of their careers to the business. Within twenty-four months of Richard's tenure as CEO, his company was suffering from a double-digit increase in voluntary attrition among team members who had been with the company between ten and twenty years. The challenge was that Richard did *care* about his people; he just wore his emotions on his sleeve and led through knee-jerk reactions, or what I call an *Authority-Apology* cadence. This is where people flex their leadership muscles by barking orders, yelling, and demanding action and will then follow up with heartfelt apologies as needed. Aggressive passive.

Richard was not aware of his contribution to the voluntary attrition, and even when presented with data from exit interviews suggesting he was, he remained in denial rather than changing his behaviors. The last I checked in with my coaching client, Richard's COO, the company had lost 5 percent market share to their most direct local competitor, including losing some top-tier talent to them.

Richard relied too heavily on a fear-based style that created a "bare minimum mentality" in which team members put in minimal effort to get by, go unnoticed, and not get yelled at. This result was not aligned with his aggressive growth goals, but he was unwilling to point his analytic mind at his own behaviors. This kind of leadership communication causes hesitancy in team members bringing problems or new ideas to the leader, and the hesitancy eventually ceases and no problems (or ideas) make their way to the top.

Having a big heart does not overcome problems caused by a big mouth.

Practice the miracle of social learning theory by imitating Gabrielle and learning from Richard's mistakes.

Root Questions

- Can you identify your primary conflict-management style? Is this style useful or harmful to your organization?
- How can appropriately regulating your Conflict RADAR sensitivity help in maintaining professionalism and effective communication?
- What role does emotional intelligence play in navigating workplace disagreements?
- How can incorporating conflict-management tools into your organizational culture benefit overall team dynamics and performance?

Missing Conversation Quick Facts

CATEGORY	ADVERSITY
Missing Conversation	Conflict RADAR
What It Does	Addresses and eliminates lingering uncertainty and anxiety related to ongoing conflicts and replaces it with a specific process to talk about the things that matter.
Why It Matters	This deceptively simple tool allows people to dissect disagreement and reframe it as an opportunity to improve.

SECTION 4

PART OF A SYSTEM

*"A wheel cannot revolve when it is
attached too tightly to the axle."*
—ANONYMOUS

Humans are skilled at convincing ourselves that we are the center of the world instead of part of a larger system. Recognizing the importance of missing conversations is a reminder that we are *one* part of a greater organizational whole. Systems matter. Developing a *systems mentality* involves consciously trying to understand the organizational world through a filter of inputs, throughputs, and outputs. Once this mindset habit is formed, leaders should then focus on managing systems rather than people.

Manage systems. Empower people. Expect big results.

Looking at organizational life through a *systems mindset* helps us understand how missing conversations can constrain a company by limiting outputs. It also highlights that information and innovation thrive when shared. By addressing missing conversations and fostering a systems mindset, leaders can prevent organizational decay and promote personal and organizational growth.

CHAPTER 38

SYSTEMS THINKING

Humans aren't wired to remember that they are part of a system; we are wired to believe that our individual thoughts, ideas, and feelings are the most important and accurate depiction of the world.

Becoming aware of missing conversations is an opportunity to remind ourselves that key conversations are a part of a greater process of productivity and that we are just one part in a much larger organizational whole.

Cultivating a systems mentality is an essential trait in developing holistic, analytical, and empathetic leadership, and it is a much simpler endeavor than many consultants and coaches make it out to be.

A system consists of inputs, throughputs, and outputs and involves the transformation of the inputs into new, and hopefully, useful things. Systems apply to making products and services and developing relationships (leadership). I do not believe leaders actually manage people. Instead, they manage systems. They should strive to empower people to do innovative and productive work within the organizational system.

Organizations are structured hierarchies that try to consistently produce an ordered, predictable outcome. But its parts are so interconnected that simply trying to "manage" a person overlooks the reality that this one person is embedded in a dynamic environment of other people with competing expectations and goals. When you drop the hammer on someone for an error on a project, that interaction has second-order effects that will most likely be invisible to you. It role-models the type of managerial behaviors that are expected, and then that person is more likely to immediately drop the hammer on their direct reports.

With regard to missing conversations, you can apply systems thinking from two vantage points:

First, missing conversations create a constraint on a system—which in this case is a team or company—because a lack of important conversations leads to suboptimal outputs. The missing inputs (conversations) limit the outputs that can be derived.

Second, information and innovation want to flourish, to be shared, to find a useful purpose. General systems thinking is now applied across all academic fields and business structures to understand how different components fit together and influence one another.

In 1968, Ludwig von Bertalanffy found that complex systems share organizing principles that can be modeled and predicted,[50] and within the last decade, biology has been recategorized as an information science. So, the study of life (biology) is both a series of systems and an information science, meaning that at our most basic cellular levels, life is made up of information that is trying to expand and reproduce itself.

All organizations follow this same logic—expand or decay. By avoiding important conversations, whether out of awareness, avoidance, or adversity, you are limiting your creative abilities as an organizational leader. If this pattern persists and grows unchecked—much like the underground network of bamboo roots—it will lead to the decay of your organization.

If you disagree and think this is hyperbole, look to extreme examples that classify informal norms related to different types of conversations. The Enron scandal was one of the largest corporate frauds and bankruptcies in US history. Team members were actively instructed not to bring Enron's leaders bad news. This limited access to a very important type of conversation that leaders (and systems) need in order to make course corrections and improve outputs.

Enron leaders sacrificed the long-term health of the company—including all of its shareholder value and pensioners' wealth—at the expense of their short-term stock price and personal-wealth accumulation. They told everyone to buy their stock—while they sold it.

Contrast that approach with what Charles Koch has created across Koch Industries, where all employees regardless of their spot in the org chart are able to make innovative operational suggestions. If their suggestions save or make the company money, the team member receives additional compensation tied to the success of their solution.

Koch also educates its employees on essential economic, entrepreneurial, and free market concepts as part of its proprietary Market-Based Management model. Charles Koch turned his personal business philosophy into an all-encompassing system and logic that guides Koch Industries. It focuses on creating value for society and giving individuals the tools to thrive.

Charles Koch personally attributes this system for making his company the second-most-valuable private company in the world.[51] In Enron and Koch, we see two different approaches to important conversations that lead to two different types of incentivized behaviors in company culture: value destruction ... and value creation.

Let's look at another example.

Leaders must decide whether to sever ties with vendors who stop providing consistent value. Human emotions and psychology influence these decisions as much as the raw numbers, and this turns what should be a straightforward business decision into a challenging choice.

Imagine a key vendor who has been a loyal stakeholder in your company's ecosystem since its founding. The owner of the vendor company personally worked weekends to make sure your company's needs were met early on in the partnership. But something changed, and now the vendor has not only stopped promptly answering calls and working on weekends, but they've started exhibiting poor performance.

Many leaders choose to avoid directly bringing this up with the vendor for far too long, usually until the financial pain covers the financial statements in red or when customers are complaining about the vendor's low-quality work.

In this case, the missing conversation is actually a *chain* (system) of conversations that should be occurring around standards, expectations, and value, both within the company among the leadership team and between the company and the vendor. But when missing, the conversational input is removed from the system and automatically limits the available outputs of this business relationship.

Let's imagine a different reality in which the leadership team doesn't wait until the financial pain is bleeding on their income statements or their customers are shouting from the rooftops. Instead, leaders choose to proactively have a difficult conversation with the vendor as soon as a problematic pattern is recognized. While uncomfortable, this honors the employment agreement, identifies the value that each is expected to receive, and clarifies the future relationship options—either continuing to work together or parting ways.

Should it be more comfortable to accept subpar work or to have a challenging conversation? Is it fair that the vendor has behaved in a way to make this type of conversation necessary?

Remember that we are all part of a system. The conversations and behaviors we bring to the workplace are also part of that system, and just because we leave certain conversations and behaviors outside of our system does not mean that they don't influence that system.

As we have discussed, bamboo grows as a complex underground system until it springs up and spreads at a rapid pace. The organizational conversations you are having are leading to different types of growth as well. I advise my clients to ensure, as much as possible, that this growth happens in the light of day and not in dark spaces inside people's heads, where resentments and negative assumptions often multiply.

Root Questions

- How does understanding that you are part of a larger system influence your approach to leadership and decision-making?
- What are some missing conversations that could be creating constraints on your organization's outputs?
- In what ways can you empower your team to engage in important conversations that foster innovation and growth?
- What lessons can be learned from examples like Enron and Koch Industries regarding the impact of missing or effective conversations on organizational success?

Missing Conversation Quick Facts

CATEGORY	PART OF A SYSTEM
Missing Conversation	Systems Thinking
What It Does	Helps leaders manage the system, empower individuals, and expect big results.
Why It Matters	Overlooking how things are interconnected will lead to mistaking symptoms for root causes, ineffective solutions, and the cyclical return of problematic behavioral patterns.

CHAPTER 39

"CONEX" AND CONVERSATIONAL COMPETENCE

"**B**AY THREE CLEAR," SHOUTED THE OIL TECHNICIAN AS he signaled it was clear to pull my car forward.

"All clear here," shouted his coworker in the next bay.

Watching the well-orchestrated and aligned activities of the Valvoline Instant Oil change team near my house, the secret sauce of this team's work became clear. Their teamwork was due to trust, which is an outcome of effective training. The "call outs" the technicians were doing are part of Valvoline's training and drive two equally important results: maintaining clear team communication and ensuring accurate work.[52]

What impressed me most was that this oil change crew demonstrated a singularity of focus around keeping their communication and work tasks synchronized. The absence of this single concept can derail a company no matter its size.

The Valvoline crew avoided unnecessary conversational expenditures (ConEx) by communicating in such an intentional, strategic, and somewhat redundant fashion. The team knew who did what, in what order, and how long each activity took. They involved customers in the conversation by explaining the oil change process and encouraging customers to watch what was happening under their hoods on the in-shop video monitoring system. This conversational approach is also a very low-pressure way to suggest additional services and upgrades. Smart sales move.

During the oil change, team members called out tasks as they were completed to signal the next team member to begin their task and allow the customer (me) to follow along. The process of interactive conversational alignment created an "oil change experience." Simple and efficient.

Companies that focus on the proactive, internal, organizational communication—the communication practices that keep teams aligned and goal-focused—create alignment at four distinct and overlapping levels:

1. From team member to their specific responsibilities.
2. From team member to the manager.
3. From team member to the team.
4. From team member to the culture.

Misalignment at any of these levels typically starts with poor (or missing) communication and a toleration of mediocrity. This quickly spirals into mounting expenses that take the form of operational friction, productivity loss, and high-performer turnover.

Thirteen minutes. That's how quickly I was headed back home after the oil change began. This symphony might not have been Mozart, but it was still music to my ears, because overlooking a simple thing like *conversational alignment* leads to death by a thousand cuts.

To minimize these small cuts, successful leaders make a regular habit of monitoring costs, increasing revenue, and enlarging margin. Small cuts have real costs. Some of them are operational expenditures (OpEx), tied to ongoing operations that keep the business running, while others are cyclical or one-off expenses for maintaining, improving, or replacing equipment, buildings, and technology (capital). These capital expenditures (CapEx) are usually implemented as a form of proactive, recurring maintenance[53] to keep machinery in good working condition or to upgrade and expand technologies, equipment, and capital.

I argue that the conversational expenditures (ConEx) are rarely accounted for, and they serve as an amplifier to both OpEx and CapEx. You can think of ConEx as "cost catalysts" that generate more costs in both of the other expense categories. Since ConEx are the costs associated with ineffective or insufficient communication, ensuring that effective and aligned communication is part of your company culture is an affordable practice to enshrine.

Specific ConEx include missed goals, finger-pointing, territoriality, drawn-out misunderstandings, misaligned projects, organizational politics, and inefficient decision-making processes. While this book is mostly focused on internal communication practices involving employees, managers, and leaders, these costs can escalate and involve external stakeholders like customers, suppliers, and regulators, as the following example demonstrates.

What is the impact of ineffective, infrequent, or missing conversations? Let me introduce an organization called Aging with Dignity, a continuous care organization for aging adults that offers independent living, assisted care, and 24/7 skilled care as part of its on-campus product lineup. The goal is to allow older adults to age in place and with dignity, as part of an energized and resident-focused community that provides as much choice and autonomy as possible.

The COO was my leadership coaching partner, and while we were focused on a much more micro aspect of organizational life (helping her address unproductive behaviors of her direct reports that were negatively impacting the culture), this vantage point gave me a front-row seat to the challenging change process that unfolded over a two-year period. As it turns out, there were many more impactful and macro reasons creating a toxic culture than the unproductive behaviors of a few employees. Aging with Dignity was previously a nonprofit company that was bought and merged with a for-profit company specializing in long-term healthcare facilities. The parent company had a regional footprint that was following a strategic-growth model via acquisitions. The new ownership did not seem prepared for the speed bumps associated with integrating Aging with Dignity into their larger model.

For starters, the average workforce tenure at this organization was eighteen years. They had a long-term and loyal team, but it was also one that was averse to change and used to doing things their way.

Second, they took on too many layers of change simultaneously. They were trying to do a product refresh of current facilities, build new facilities, add additional medical (memory care) and leisure services (concierge-style amenities), add new in-room technologies for residents, overhaul nursing and dietary policies and procedures, and adapt the entire organization to the new culture, which emphasized fast pace, centralized problem-solving, and major cost cutting.

Third, the post-integration leadership team was a combination of managers from the parent company and three leaders who stayed on to guide the community through the change (including my partner).

It quickly became apparent that transparent communication, respect, and clarity were not high priorities for the leadership team members from the parent organization. A web of problems emerged within thirty days of the deal closing, and there were several major impacts.

Typical voluntary staff attrition in nursing homes is 52 percent,[54] and my client's organization experienced up to 100 percent turnover in certain segments of their business while navigating the change. This meant they were having to replace an entire team of staff members in certain areas of their healthcare facility. This was a huge ordeal for three reasons:

1. The leaders weren't prepared to replace so many positions so quickly, as the average staff member tenure had previously been eighteen years.
2. There was a relatively lean talent pool in the surrounding community to draw from.

3. This organization had to meet state-regulated compliance guidelines in terms of staff-to-resident ratios.

From the few exit interviews that were conducted, there was a resounding theme: Employees were being kept in the dark, there was no feedback from leadership, and team members felt the new leaders were adversarial and unsupportive. The productivity of those who did stick around was negatively impacted, with the common result of "winning" more responsibility without additional pay or promotions.

Productivity plunged, as measured by the number of residents that nursing staff medically and socially connected with daily, and miscommunications led to repeated tasks, errors, and wasted time in clarifications. Deadlines were rarely hit and when they were, it was with an announcement of a new deadline. This also had direct implications for the residents' health and wellness.

A subtle but devastating hit to company culture (and financial statements) happens when employee morale declines, everyone knows it, and no one does anything about it. Aging with Dignity saw its internal employee engagement scores go from an "A" to a "D+" and its Net Promoter Scores drop from greater than 80 over a five-year period to a series of negative scores.

Maintaining high Net Promoter Scores is crucial because the survey asks two key questions: (a) would a person recommend the workplace to friends and family looking for jobs? and (b) would a person recommend the company's products and services to friends and family?

When these results drop from *excellent* to *problematic* in such a short time span, there is a major organizational problem that could potentially threaten the existence of the business.

In addition to the strife from poor internal organizational practices and a suboptimal communication environment, there are external factors that can negatively impact a business as well. In this case, communication with residents and their family member decision-makers also suffered during this poorly managed change process. Misunderstandings and insufficient attempts at explaining the changes—such as how the building refresh and planned construction would impact the daily lives of the aging adults—led to dissatisfaction of current residents, loss of future residents (i.e., people withdrew their entrance fees/deposits), and reputational damage that was evident in mediocre fundraising (i.e., several recurring donors stopped giving).

ConEx has both qualitative and quantitative costs associated with it. You can calculate time loss by adding up the hours spent on dealing with misunderstandings, clarifying instructions, and redoing work, and multiply that by the hourly wage of the people doing the "fixing."

This can be applied to people on salaries as well. Just calculate their hourly wage by dividing their salary by 2,000.[55] However, this doesn't even include the emotional and psychological stress and strain from poorly managed change projects. When people are under immense psychological and emotional strain in the workplace, they are rarely bringing their best selves to work each morning (and definitely not back home), and this amplifies the financial and operational challenges. When people are emotionally exhausted, they aren't going to be optimal problem solvers.

The financial impact to an organization adds up quickly beyond the time loss and labor expense, because project delays, errors, and reduced productivity also punish financial statements. Finally, turnover costs are often a huge *hidden* expense, with employers paying between six and nine months' worth of salary to replace a full-time employee.[56] In addition, team members who stick around and pick up the slack get incrementally disgruntled over time, leading to new problems and costs.

But all is not lost. There are several strategies companies can enact to reduce the negative impact of ConEx, prevent the outcomes experienced in this case, and increase a company's conversational competence. First and foremost, leaders need to assess their current internal organizational communication practices and whether those practices are tethered to company mission, vision, values, and strategy, or if they are the brainchild of a single leader. The following prompts are useful for that discussion:

- In what direction does information flow across your organization?
- Does information get to who needs it in a timely fashion?
- Are there recurring bottlenecks, and if so, are they due to poor procedures, technology, or people?
- As a leadership team, where are we on the scale of openness to innovation?
- Are we resilient in the face of disagreement, or do we avoid it?

- Do we have right-sized communication tools and procedures that fit our culture?

Once the current state of conversational competence is understood, then leaders should prioritize and road map the problems to address. Common solutions often emerge, such as investing in appropriate communication technologies or eliminating confusing and redundant communication technologies. These simple solutions help with alignment and knowledge transfer. But new technologies and refined communication norms are not a cure-all. You must also make sure people know how and when to use these technologies and new procedures, and that can only come through training and accountability.

At its core, training is really the elimination of choice to create habits that save time and create efficiency. It is about building muscle memory, so people don't have to think through every decision or opportunity—they can just respond correctly. Companies need to provide internal training on effective communication techniques and best practices, ideally facilitated by the managers and leaders at the company.[57] No one knows a company's mission, vision, values, and strategy like its leaders and managers, which, according to Andy Grove, co-founder of Intel, is exactly why they are the ones who should conduct as many types of technical and soft-skills training as possible. Companies also need to implement regular feedback mechanisms to ensure continuous improvement, and this feedback should cut both ways across the org chart.

There are many well-known companies who exhibit conversational competence and strategically avoid escalating ConEx, including 3M, United Rentals, United Waste Systems, XPO, Netflix, Amazon, Blackrock, and Apple (just to name a few). These companies focus on establishing clear project and task objectives, consistently communicate those objectives to the appropriate stake-holders, and then schedule regular check-ins to ensure alignment and promptly address issues. These recurring *huddles*, as I call them, should be brief and laser-focused on communication clarity, problem-solving, and identifying what's missing.

Do not allow tangential issues to take over huddles, because tangents are "time thieves" that slowly sap every-one's energy. The companies on the list above also document key decisions, action items, deadlines, and task ownership, to reinforce alignment and prevent simple misunderstandings.

When ritualized, these simple and brief conversations prevent the thousand cuts that bleed out a balance sheet. Much like the Valvoline technician teams, these Fortune 100 leadership teams build and reinforce a culture that values organizational communication. They know it leads to alignment—and results.

Root Questions

- What are the potential costs associated with poor communication (ConEx) in your organization, and how can they be mitigated?
- How can regular, intentional communication practices prevent misalignment and operational friction within your leadership team?
- In what ways can training and accountability enhance conversational competence?
- What steps can you take to foster a culture that values proactive and strategic communication, like the examples of successful companies mentioned in this chapter?

Missing Conversation Quick Facts

CATEGORY	PART OF A SYSTEM
Missing Conversation	Conversational Competence and ConEx
What It Does	Ensures that effective and aligned communication is a daily part of your company culture and operations, an intelligent business practice and system to enshrine.
Why It Matters	ConEx acts as a cost catalyst that generates more costs in both OpEx and CapEx by leading to missed goals, blame, territoriality, misaligned projects, organizational politics, and inefficient decision-making processes.

CHAPTER 40

OFF TO THE RACES

MUCH LIKE RACE CAR DRIVERS, BUSINESS LEADERS MUST monitor a variety of conditions and be constantly scanning for emerging hazards.

As we saw in the previous chapter, identifying and reducing conversational expenditures (ConEx) is crucial in our organizations. And reducing ConEx means identifying the missing conversations.

So, ask yourself, *What key conversations are missing? Is my gut telling me we should talk about something even though it's uncomfortable?* These conversations might be a little tense, awkward, or unpleasant—and they will briefly slow down project pace—but they serve an important function, like a pace car in professional racing.

Spectators do not attend races to watch the pace car. When you get home, you don't share stories about the pace car. The pace car driver receives no glory. Yet the pace car serves several important and underappreciated functions that maintain the integrity of the race system and are integral to its eventual conclusion.

The pace car controls the start of the race and lets drivers warm up their tires, brakes, and engines, giving drivers a feel for the track conditions. Gaining this "feel for the track" lets drivers eventually push the pedal to the metal. Is the course slick? Is it sticky on certain turns? The pace car helps prevent chaotic car wrecks and pileups, and when chaos does emerge, it's the pace car that returns to the track to create or re-establish order from that chaos.

Pace cars provide safety during cautions, so when there is an accident or hazardous conditions like debris or weather, the pace car slows down the field of drivers to ensure they can continue the race. By maintaining the positions of the cars after a hazard, the pace car makes sure safety is enforced and the rank-ordered sequence of drivers is preserved. Finally, in certain types of races like endurance racing, pace cars help to manage event timing, making sure the race does not take too long or end too quickly.

It's a thankless job, but the pace car driver prioritizes the safety of everyone else on the track and plays an indispensable role in the winner's victory.

The same is true for leaders who do the similarly thankless job of thinking strategically about organizational communication.

Systematically addressing ConEx and slowing things down on the "first lap" of a project prepares the team for a safe, smooth, and fast race to the finish line. Team members are able to work faster, gaining speed from improved team alignment, goal clarity, work-task purpose, clearer standards and benchmarks, better project outcomes, and enhanced employee and customer satisfaction.

We usually love it when projects are speeding along to completion, but it can't be all pedal-to-the-metal from start to finish. That's like a race car that only has one gear—full throttle. That's not an asset; it's a liability with a guaranteed crash-and-burn ending.

I love driving, and I love driving fast, both on motorcycles and in cars. I was lucky enough to attend a Corvette performance-driving academy outside of Las Vegas, and my main takeaway was counterintuitive: You win races by how you brake.

Everyone floors it in the straightaways, but races are won and lost in how early and hard a driver brakes when approaching turns. Braking sooner and harder allows them to unwind the steering wheel and accelerate out of each turn.

It's the same in organizational life. Pumping the brakes at times feels like you are going too slow and will prevent goal achievement. But that is very different than asking a driver to get out of the car; you are simply ensuring wheel alignment, calibrated navigation, and preventing people from smacking against the wall from not braking hard enough.[58]

Industry-leading companies operationalize strategies that minimize ConEx and emphasize the long-term benefits of *briefly* slowing down to increase their pace for the remainder of the race. And companies with internal organizing practices that create conversational competence are companies that win races.[59]

Root Questions

- How can you create balance between maintaining a fast project pace and ensuring thorough communication and alignment?
- In what ways can adopting a "pace car" mentality improve your leadership communication behaviors?
- What are some examples of situations where pumping the brakes could lead to better long-term results for your organization?

Missing Conversation Quick Facts

CATEGORY	PART OF A SYSTEM
Missing Conversation	Slow Down to Speed Up
What It Does	Systematically addressing ConEx and slowing things down on the "first lap" of a project prepares the team for a safe, smooth, and fast race to the finish line.
Why It Matters	Team members are able to gain speed from improved team alignment, goal clarity, work-task purpose, and clearer standards and benchmarks.

CHAPTER 41

THE BEGINNER'S MINDSET

"**D**O WE HAVE A CLEAR STRATEGY?" THE CEO ASKED HER leadership team.

The team was facing unprecedented challenges in the market as automated technologies had changed their business model and allowed competitors to eat away at their local market share. She gave time for her team to think, and eventually the CFO and HR Director both reluctantly said, "Grow or die."

"That's a good start," the CEO responded, "but what's missing?" she tossed back to the team.

The COO instantly chimed in, "*How* and *where* we need to grow based on where we are currently."

This team member was starting to uncover the most important conversation a team needs to have regarding strategy, and that involves *how* to grow.

He continued, "There's a lot that has changed, and there's a lot we don't know. If we don't want to lose our market share, we need to build a formal plan."

This company was in the business of precision injection molding, which is an extremely technical process that produces complex plastic components. It is a capital-intensive business and requires specialized technical competencies from its workforce. The organization had invented a unique manufacturing process that increased production efficiency, but their intellectual property had recently expired and competitors were copying it. Competitors were also heavily investing in CapEx projects to add state-of-the-art automation and robotics.

The leadership team was faced with a fork in the road: put their heads down, work hard, keep doing what they had been doing, and try to grow their way out of the situation using the same game plan as before—or discuss what had changed in the market environment and how they needed to adapt to those changes.

They chose the second option.

Over the course of their next five leadership team meetings, the leaders engaged in organic strategic planning activities. They conducted a SWOT analysis to understand their current state, each leadership team member conducted market research on competitors and customers, and they also conducted a lite version of Michael Porter's Five Forces analysis.

The combination of these activities created a data-driven approach to decision-making that allowed them to identify their competitive advantages and articulate what made them unique from their competitors. They learned what their market currently wanted and did research to learn what it might want over the next twelve to thirty-six months.

In this version of the scenario from the opening scene of the book, the CEO and COO adopted the beginner's mindset. This is a powerful form of thinking that frees a person from carrying the "burden of expertise" and leverages the freedom of being a student, of being open to learning, of admitting you don't have all the answers.

The beginner's mindset is aware of limits and boundaries, fosters collaborative problem-solving, believes in continuous learning and feedback loops, and actively shares knowledge through training and mentoring. This mindset helps us set aside expectations and our current knowledge to create a gap we can fill with *new* data, ideas, and knowledge. It is less about "unlearning" and more an awareness to engage in a thought experiment to bracket our knowledge and experience and learn from what's in front of us.

It is captured in the phrase, "I want to learn. Teach me."

The leadership team in this story collectively embraced the spirit of the beginner's mindset because the CEO was vulnerable and honest enough to admit she didn't have all the answers. The team needed to figure them out together. In the end, they worked with a facilitator (me) to help structure and record their planning process, but they put in the work to refine and build their company strategy.

The ancient Greek Stoic philosopher Epictetus, a self-educated former slave who wrote *The Discourses*, taught that unchecked self-worth and narcissism destroys a person's life purpose. It distracts from problems in the outside world and encourages them to look inward too often. It fatigues us by spreading our resources too thin, where our ambition or vanity persuades us to tackle too many problems at once. Epictetus encouraged people to adopt the beginner's mindset to avoid these problems.

Being a leader, founder, owner, or manager in a company comes with responsibility. People know they must drive results to grow a business, and they hopefully stretch themselves and their team members in productive ways during the process. Unfortunately, many people in positions of organizational responsibility also believe they must have *all* the answers *all* the time. They think they should be viewed as an omnipotent subject matter expert, project confidence and certainty, and be an unwavering tree of knowledge.

Of course, there is some truth to this, because individual leaders need to exhibit confidence, certainty, and expertise. But they need to do so within reasonable bounds, being sure to remember to build these traits in the team, not just in themselves.

What they really need is courage. Courage to admit they don't know everything, but more importantly, courage to believe the team can solve more problems and add more value than any individual team member.[60] They need the courage to act like the giant timber bamboo, to help their team pump the brakes on taking immediate action based on a false sense of projected certainty, and instead dig into the tough conversations, figuring out what things mean to each person on the team. When done well, establishing deep roots up front with a leadership team through key conversations takes time but leads to explosive growth later.

When conversations are left untended and neglected, whether due to lack of awareness, avoidance, or adversity, invasive organizational practices will take root. And once formed, habits are hard to change or eliminate. Just as bamboo is a multifunctional plant when it is properly contained by laying out boundaries and barriers, conversations (and their outcomes) are multifunctional and productive when preceded with useful boundaries, disclaimers, and expectations.

The beginner's mindset is empowering for two parties: the person adopting the mindset, and the person/people doing the teaching.

My wife and I were inspired by some good friends who tear it up on the dance floor together, so we signed up for salsa classes. It was so liberating to surrender certainty, to enjoy being a student again, shooting my hand up to ask questions and asking the instructor to demonstrate certain moves. To improve my dance moves, I sought (a lot) of feedback. I removed the weight of responsibility and status and instead focused on learning a skill and increasing intimacy with my wife. Win-win.

Brené Brown has popularized the significance of vulnerable communication and humble leadership. I admire her work, which effectively repackages timeless concepts into actionable insights for millions of people. The Stoics would thank her. She is brilliant, and I integrate many of her concepts and tools into my coaching partnerships. I believe ideas should be played with, expanded, and modified, so I have used her ideal of the brave, authentic, and vulnerable leader as a foundation for further differentiating types of organizational humility.

When I talk about cultivating humility in the workplace with my clients, we break it down into three different types of humility—*practical humility*, *project humility*, and *people humility*. While the categories are not mutually exclusive

Three Types of Humility
Embodying the Beginner's Mindset

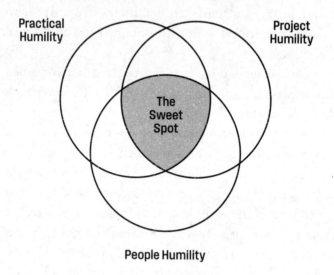

Figure 7. Hitting the crosshairs of the three types
of humility is the goal, and it is rare.

and have overlap, as exhibited in the image, all three categories embody the beginner's mindset.

Practical humility is about recognizing intellectual, cognitive, and technical limitations. It is about knowing your swim lane and authoritatively sharing your knowledge and teaching others when a problem is in your lane. When someone seeks your advice, refrain from acting like a know-it-all. Leaders with practical humility consistently exhibit the following characteristics*:

• Willingness to learn and adapt

---

* I used ChatGPT to help flush out the following three lists of bullet points.

- Willingness to seek out subject matter experts with true technical skills
- Willingness to build a team that complements their knowledge and skill gaps
- Openness to new ideas, evidence, and viewpoints
- Striving to think and act in terms of probabilities rather than absolutes or certainties
- Cultivating an environment and mindset of continuous improvement and innovation
- Embracing calculated risk-taking

Project humility is about recognizing decision-making limits, using small failures and mistakes as learning opportunities, knowing that you always have only a partial view of the future, and understanding that strategy must embrace a degree of uncertainty. Leaders with project humility:

- Position the subject matter experts to make specialized decisions and the leadership team to make enterprise decisions
- Foster a deliberation culture that honors each other's expertise
- Maintain a healthy tension of making decisions driven by expertise while seeking and listening to outside viewpoints
- Acknowledge course corrections and mistakes
- View failures as signals to investigate leading and lagging indicators
- Listen to the team, to the market, and to competitors
- Know that adaptability is the essence of effective strategy

People humility is about exhibiting emotional awareness, communication competence, and ethical mindful-
ness. These soft skills are often juxtaposed against hard
skills or technical skills, but I think that is a false dichotomy.
Soft skills are hard skills. In fact, they are usually more difficult to train than technical skills.

Leaders who have people humility know when to lead
and when to manage, when to inspire and when to give a
directive, when to "decide and announce," and when to
crowdsource ideas with the team. They have mastered the
science of organizing their business with the art of people
development.

Leaders with people humility:
- Have an intuitive feel for when to take charge, influ-
ence, direct, connect, and inspire.
- Believe the team can get more accomplished than the
leader alone.
- Understand and use emotional dimensions of
communication.
- Exhibit authentic empathy and curiosity for others'
experiences.
- Know how to quickly build connections and trust
- Connect an individual's role to the big picture (systems
thinker).
- Lead by the Platinum Rule,[61] not the Golden Rule
- Prefer trust and loyalty as primary incentive mecha-
nisms but know when to use fear.
- Discuss the moral and ethical dimensions of organiza-
tional decisions as needed.
- Commit to doing what's right, especially when it's
challenging.

- Move beyond reflective thinking to build reflexive communication skills, giving them the ability to pause and adapt in the moment.

Leaders who consistently exhibit all three forms of organizational humility are written into the history books. Those who demonstrate two of the three types build market-leading companies and are role models in their industry. Those who only exhibit one type of organizational humility can have a successful organization but are falling short of their full potential.

How's that humble pie taste?

Root Questions

- How does holding on to the "burden of expertise" limit your ability to adapt and innovate?
- In what areas can adopting a beginner's mindset enhance your leadership?
- How do you currently handle small failures and mistakes in team decision-making processes?
- What practices can you implement to cultivate practical, project, and people humility in your leadership approach?
- When was the last time you admitted you didn't have all the answers, and how did it impact your team?

Missing Conversation Quick Facts

CATEGORY	PART OF A SYSTEM
Missing Conversation	The Beginner's Mindset
What It Does	Frees a person from carrying the "burden of expertise" and leverages the freedom of being open to learning, of admitting you don't have all the answers, and of experimenting.
Why It Matters	When consistently striving for the beginner's mindset, a leader will exhibit three types of humility: practical, project, and people.

CULTIVATING CONVERSATIONS

THE MOST IMPORTANT CONVERSATIONS WE SHOULD BE having in the workplace are usually the ones that are missing. This is because leaders aren't aware of what they could be talking about, are actively avoiding difficult topics, or are distracted by adversity. When key conversations are neglected or are conducted haphazardly, that leads to unproductive results.

It's not that leaders don't try to have essential conversations with their teams and key stakeholders. It's just that the whirlwind of work takes over and distracts them before they make this process a habit. Many organizational leadership teams do have challenging but effective conversations and make high-quality decisions, but this communication excellence is rarely operationalized into their organizational culture. Whether it is human nature, the appeal of guru-suggested guidelines, or some other phenomenon, leaders often make decisions using criteria that are ambiguous or jargon-laden. It sounds smart but lacks clarity, and this leads to fruitless debates and territorial defensiveness, as everyone tries to decipher the meaning and guard their part of the org chart.

Leaders can be strategic about using ambiguous communication intentionally, as Eric Eisenberg discussed in his seminal article,[62] but this assumes that communication is actually occurring, that messages are being shared. Ambiguous messaging can serve a purpose in an organizational setting because it can help with complex change when competing interests and goals are involved. It is hard to make a similar argument for what conversations don't occur, what messages are missing, and the solutions and challenges that are not discussed.

While ambiguous communication is better than missing conversations, it still robs decision-makers of the ability to distinguish useful decisions from problematic ones and to develop a movement toward results. Conversations that involve too much ambiguity or too much jargon encourage people to focus on semantics instead of which solutions make the most sense.

As Shane Parrish says, "If you can't be away [from your job], it doesn't mean that you're indispensable or a supremely competent leader; it means that you are an incompetent communicator at best,"[63] or a bottleneck power seeker at worst.

I make the same argument about conversational presence. If your team or company cannot function without you there to ask questions, bring up topics, or create communication stability, that is a liability, not an asset.

As we draw to a close, I'd like to suggest a four-step process for overcoming the invasive problems that arise from missing conversations. You cannot harvest fruit from a barren garden or just after planting a seed. Nor can you harvest innovative ideas from missing conversations. The following four high-level guidelines will help you cultivate a healthy conversational garden and prevent invasive ideas from growing underground (in people's heads) and popping up in unwanted areas.

First is *courage*. While this begins as an individual attribute, courageous communication and embracing vulnerability should also be baked into organizational culture. This treats the soil so results can bloom.

Second is *curiosity*, another individual characteristic that leaders should strive to make part of organizational structure. Curiosity is a necessary quality of a strategic mindset, a big-picture thinker, and an adaptable organization.[64] This is what tills the garden.

Third is *learning to ask better questions*.[65] This is the operational aspect of making sure your conversational garden doesn't remain barren. Focusing on *what kinds* of questions to ask is a tactical approach that will produce results that are most likely inconsistent if they aren't tied to a specific strategy.

Fourth is *follow-up and follow-through*. This is where useful ideas are harvested and implemented, rotten ideas are discarded, relationships are repaired, and trust is re-established. Taking action on the ideas that emerge from the previously missing conversations will help grow organizational results and relationships.

Conversations are like gardens. They can be alive and lush, full of fruit and energy. Or they can be sparse and barren, overgrown with weeds, producing no nourishment.

Organizational conversations are similar. In the introduction I said that conversations are like giant timber bamboo, the fast-growing grass that first forms an underground network before springing up—seemingly out of nowhere—and growing at a rapid pace for several months.

Now imagine a garden of giant timber bamboo the size of a football field. This can be curated and used to become (and build) a beautiful structure, or it can become an overgrown, invasive nightmare, much like kudzu has become in the southern United States.

Conversations often occur in team settings, and teams are alive, organic organisms that adapt to their environments. Leadership teams shape their environments and can grow them in two possible directions. The wrong direction grows confusion, false agreement, surface-level alignment, and private resentments. The correct direction finds the missing (important) topics, builds trust, engages in candid communication, and values effective confrontation.

The latter list drives results; the former list prevents them.

The right conversations are integral to leading your organization in the right direction.

To plant the seeds of effective conversations, you first need to become aware of which ones are missing. Then, quickly get to growing them in the right direction.

ACKNOWLEDGMENTS

THANK YOU TO MY WIFE, KIZZY, AND OUR CHILDREN, Claudia and Ben, for extending me the grace and patience to complete this project in the evenings and on the weekends.

Thank you to all my consulting and coaching clients over the years who have worked with me to improve their leadership communication behaviors and organizational structures. I have easily learned as much from all of you as you have from me.

Finally, a huge thanks to my team at Forefront Books, specifically Jen, Justin, Allen, Landon, and Lauren. Your patience with my pushed deadlines and your expertise in turning muddled ideas into polished stories have helped bring this book to life. Any positive future actions that my readers take is a direct reflection of this team. Any errors or issues in the book are solely my responsibility.

SPARK THE DISCUSSION™

Take Action, Learn More

Scan the following QR code to learn more about Spark The Discussion's solutions to professional development:

About the Author

ZACH "DR. Z" SCHAEFER IS A LEADERSHIP COACH, consultant, and mediator, as well as a co-owner of The Post Sports Bar & Grill, a thriving sports bar chain based in St. Louis. With an impressive career spanning both academia and entrepreneurship, Dr. Z has dedicated himself to helping hundreds of organizations bridge the gap between strategy and execution by aligning people and business goals.

As a thought leader, Dr. Z's insights have been featured in the *Harvard Business Review*, CNBC, and *Fast Company*. A retired tenured professor and certified mediator, he brings a wealth of knowledge to his clients, fostering both personal and organizational development that enables leaders to build cohesive, resilient teams. Dr. Z speaks extensively both domestically and internationally on leadership and organizational transformation.

Beyond consulting and coaching, he serves as Chief Culture Officer at The Post Sports Bar & Grill, where he applies his communication-centered philosophy to a team of over 160 employees. Driven by his mission to serve as an action catalyst through communication, Dr. Z's work consistently delivers impactful, sustainable results.

Notes

1   "*Phyllostachys Vivax*: Giant Timber Bamboo," Boone County Arboretum, https://bcarboretum.org/plants/genus/Phyllostachys/species/vivax.

2   Marco Iacovoni, *Mirroring People: The New Science of How We Connect with Others* (Farrar, Straus and Giroux, 2008).

3   Lee Ross, "The Intuitive Psychologist and His Shortcomings: Distortions in the Attribution Process," in *Advances in Experimental Social Psychology* vol. 10 (Academic Press, 1977), 173–220.

4   Organizational politics is usually discussed in a negative light, but it should be mentioned that this concept is part of human nature. People are political animals who want to pursue and achieve power, a feeling of control, mastery, and authority over their job or company, so it makes sense they will use influence tactics to enhance that power. The point is to be aware of the type of organizational politics at your organization, to know how people play the game, and to prevent as many negative consequences of it as possible. It can never be eliminated because it ties into what makes us human.

5   We have a list of twenty common tactics we have identified that people use to play organizational politics. It is important to be aware of these games so you know when they are being played and to try to eliminate them, because they are rarely concerned with driving organizational results. Email us for the list: info@sparkthediscussion.com.

6   This is not referring to the "relief valve" complaining that we all do from time to time to clear our *frustration cache*. It is important to refrain from doing relief valve complaining too often, to keep it brief when we do it, and to only do so with a trusted confidant. But it is necessary and healthy to periodically clear the cache so we can fill that brain space with more productive ideas and information.

7 This makes me think of the lowest common denominator of citizenship—"I pay my taxes"—or the lowest common denominators of decency—"I didn't scream at the person or get violent with them."

8 Peter Attia, MD, with Bill Gifford, *Outlive: The Science and Art of Longevity* (Harmony, 2023).

9 Confrontation communication includes the messaging, tone, timing, and style we use when confronting someone. This type of communication typically involves disagreement and/or sharing an opinion that will most likely make someone else uncomfortable, especially when delivered with poor messaging, timing, and tone. People with expertise in confrontation communication know when to pick their battles, and when they choose to confront others, it is performed with tact and communication competence. They can consistently drive the result they are looking for even during difficult conversations.

10 I want to clarify that I am not referring to compliance procedures as part of risk management practices, auditing, or compliance as a department. Clearly, compliance has an important function in an organizational setting in general, but not as the guiding philosophy of what could be an impactful conversation to change behaviors.

11 To complete a no-commitment (free), five-minute simple survey on human motivation, email us at info@sparkthediscussion.com. The data demonstrates how these tools will positively impact your workplace.

12 See Morris, Grehl, Rutter, Mehta, and Rustwater's (2022) paper in *Cambridge University Press* that discusses how personality traits (part of internal drives) tend to be more stable and consistent across different situations than specific behaviors, which are often situationally dependent. https://www.cambridge.org/core/journals/psychological-medicine/article/on-what-motivates-us-a-detailed-review-of-intrinsic-v-extrinsic-motivation/3FC35CD80D991744CD764AF2FBCD3BBB. See also William Moulton Marston, *Emotions of Normal People* (Andesite Press, 2015).

13 Andy Grove, *Only the Paranoid Survive: How to Exploit the Crisis Points That Challenge Every Company* (Doubleday Business, 1996).

14 Amy Chua, Jed Rubenfeld, *The Triple Package: Why Groups Rise and Fall in America* (Penguin, 2014).

15 I use many of Porter's ideas when doing strategic planning and strategic thinking with my clients. For those who like to think conceptually and analytically, I recommend his book, *Competitive Strategy: Techniques for Analyzing Industries and Competitors* (Free Press, 1998). For a more practical

approach to his ideas, I recommend Joan Magretta's book, *Understanding Michael Porter: The Essential Guide to Competition and Strategy* (Harvard Business Review Press, 2011), where she gives an overview of his key ideas and frameworks and how organizations can apply them.

16 James A. Baker III, with Steve Fiffer, *Work Hard, Study ... and Keep Out of Politics!* (New York: G.P. Putnam's Sons, 2006).

17 Dell discusses this in his book, *Play Nice But Win: A CEO's Journey from Founder to Leader* (Portfolio, 2021).

18 It was actually Mark Fields, the former CEO of Ford, who popularized this phrase when he used it in the context of Ford's corporate culture. Fields personally attributed it to Drucker, suggesting that Drucker emphasized the importance of culture in driving organizational success.

19 Legal risk-based ignorance is when organizational leaders shy away from trying things out for fear that the actions could create legal risks. It is important to reduce this knowledge gap by talking to people with legal knowledge (both attorneys and people in your industry with experience), but also to remember that every new and innovative behavior and decision will have embedded risks. And there is no reward without risk.

20 If this interests you, check out the Hawthorne Studies and the Hawthorne Effect. This is where people alter their behaviors when they know they are being observed, especially if the observer has control or influence over incentives and evaluations. While some scholars have questioned the validity of the data from the original studies, the workplace takeaway from the research is useful: People change the way they act when being watched (especially by a boss).

21 The savings cited here were extrapolated from a survey sample to represent a one-hundred-person firm and a five-thousand-person firm. Steven G. Rogelberg, *The Cost of Unnecessary Meeting Attendance*, Otter.ai/UNC Charlotte (2022), https://20067454.fs1.hubspotusercontent-na1.net/hubfs/20067454/Report_The%20Cost%20of%20Unnecessary%20Meeting%20Attendance.pdf, 19.

22 For excellent discussions of risk that pertain to decision-making and life, I recommend three books: the former progressional poker player and cognitive-behavioral science author Annie Duke's *Thinking in Bets: Making Smarter Decisions When You Don't Have All the Facts* (Portfolio, 2018); one of the greatest investors in the world, Howard Marks's *The Most Important Thing: Uncommon Sense for the Thoughtful Investor* (Columbia Business School, 2011); and the former intelligence analyst turned author, blogger,

and speaker Shane Parrish's *Clear Thinking: Turning Ordinary Moments into Extraordinary Results* (Portfolio, 2023).

23 I have my clients use David Fields's decision-rights tool called *FARCI*: Final Authority, Approval, Recommend, Consult, Inform; www.davidafields.com.

24 Hertzberg discussed his theory in two books: *The Motivation to Work* and *One More Time*.

25 There are psychological reasons for this that are beyond the scope of this book. But if your primary communication style is to always accommodate and give in to others during discussions or disagreements, that is not a healthy communication practice.

26 "The Bubble," the fifteenth episode in the third season of the NBC series *30 Rock*.

27 Steve Jobs always talked about how he was most proud of all the projects and opportunities Apple didn't pursue. He understood the power of *no*. See Walter Isaacson's biography *Steve Jobs* (Simon & Schuster, 2011) for a more thorough discussion of this concept.

28 Freek Vermeulen, "Many Strategies Fail Because They're Not Actually Strategies," *Harvard Business Review*, November 8, 2017, hbr.org/2017/11/many-strategies-fail-because-theyre-not-actually-strategies.

29 We have a tool called *Line of Sight* for measuring leadership alignment in six key areas that are shown to lead to consistent execution when leadership teams are properly aligned, and lead to execution misfires when they aren't aligned. Contact us to learn more: info@sparkthediscussion.com.

30 Dr. Furey is a talented clinical psychologist who helped me identify and improve in the areas of impatience, frustration, and anger. He revealed my blind spots in how these concepts are related for me, created trip wires to short-circuit my explosion process, and improved my quality of life at home and work. And I love that my anger counselor is named Dr. *Furey*!

31 Brené Brown's work focuses on this topic, both the courage to be vulnerable and the power of vulnerability. My ideas as presented in this chapter are more fully explained and explored by her work, and I endorse and appreciate her approach and philosophy.

32 Research shows that having team members first write down their individual rankings before sharing with the group can improve the accuracy and objectivity of the final rankings, because it avoids members trying to match the most influential or senior person in the room. See: Cheng-Ju Hsieh, Mario Fifić, and Cheng-Ta Yang, "A New Measure of Group Decision-Making Efficiency," *Cognitive Research: Principles and Implications*

5, no. 45 (2020), https://cognitiveresearchjournal.springeropen.com/articles/10.1186/s41235-020-00244-3.

33 *We Bought a Zoo*, directed by Cameron Crowe (20th Century Fox, 2011).

34 I am a self-described administrative minimalist. I am always encouraging my clients to eliminate rules and processes, when warranted, and instead opt for direct, face-to-face communication. My guideline is that the less rules and paperwork, the happier the culture.

35 If American banks really want to fulfill their mission and connect their clients to the resources they need to be successful, they could empower branch managers with the appropriate authority and training to solve simple customer needs. A depersonalized banking experience is antithetical to their entire business model, which is supposed to be built on trust. This impersonal, transactional approach to financial business will one day bite them in the bottom-line butt if they don't guard against it.

36 Behavioral issues that relate to poor attitude and personality quirks are much harder to talk about than performance issues. Because with the latter, most companies have more objective measurement data to discuss the problem and what needs to change. Discussing attitude/personality change requires more nuance.

37 The psychologist Irving Janis created this concept in 1971 in his paper, "Victims of Groupthink: A Psychological Study of Foreign-Policy Decisions and Fiascoes," and he actually chose the term "groupthink" as a parallel to George Orwell's term "doublethink."

38 Laurence Peter discusses this concept in his 1969 book, *The Peter Principle* (William Morrow & Co.).

39 See Danielle Li, Kelly Shue, Alan Benson, "Promotions and the Peter Principle," VoxEU, April 24, 2019, https://cepr.org/voxeu/columns/promotions-and-peter-principle.

40 I have learned that many leaders don't have a firm grasp of how to lead from financial statements. They don't know how to look at a P&L, Balance Sheet, or Cash Flow statement and make operational decisions (to drive daily behaviors on their team) or strategic decisions (how to better allocate capital; company strategy). We put together a simple ninety-minute workshop called *Leading from Financial Statements* to solve this issue.

41 Think of this as *conversational preventative maintenance*.

42 Accountability expert and keynote speaker Sam Silverstein discusses the relationship between accountability and responsibility in his speeches and his books *No More Excuses* and *Non-Negotiable*. He says we are *accountable*

to people and *responsible* for things, and I agree with him. Sam is a generous (and busy) person who chose to take several meetings with me when I was getting my speaking career off the ground ten years ago. I appreciated his time and knowledge and try to pass it on whenever possible.

43 This concept comes from Kant's extremely dense and esoteric book, *Groundwork of the Metaphysics of Morals*. A must-read for all newly promoted managers.

44 We met Dr. Robert Furey a few chapters ago. He's the therapist who has helped me manage my natural preferences for impatience, frustration, and anger.

45 I want to clarify that I received permission to include this chapter both from the Vistage member and the chair.

46 I am one of the lucky ones!

47 I agree with Howard Marks in that there is a difference between pessimism and skepticism, which he outlines in his book, *Mastering the Market Cycle: Getting the Odds on Your Side* (Harper Business, 2021). Marks says that pessimism is when people can only see the downside of an opportunity and always expect the worst. Skepticism is questioning accepted wisdom, remaining a critical thinker based on emergent facts, and being leery of claims to truth without proper analysis. Skeptics can question environments that become too optimistic or too pessimistic. Optimists only see opportunity and exude confidence, pessimists only see risks and feel insecure, and skeptics will question both situations until the truth emerges based on data.

48 See the 2022 book *Talent* by Tyler Cowen and Daniel Gross that discusses how to attract and retain top talent. While their focus and experience is in the tech sector, there are some techniques and tools that cut across industries.

49 I have been formally mediating disputes and conflicts since 2008 and I still use written notes in every situation. I can't predict what people will do or say, and my notes keep me focused on what's important: helping them find common ground and move on with their lives.

50 Ludwig von Bertalanffy, *General System Theory: Foundations, Development, Applications* (New York: George Braziller, 1968).

51 Charles G. Koch, *The Science of Success: How Market-Based Management Built the World's Largest Private Company* (Hoboken, NJ: John Wiley & Sons, 2007).

52 The information in this chapter has been adapted from a 2019 blog post I

wrote on my website: https://www.sparkthediscussion.com/the-biggest-threat-youve-never-thought-of-the-oil-change-symphony/.

53 The lines get blurry between CapEx and OpEx when an expense is of a "sporadically recurring" variety, because you could argue the costs are required to keep operations functioning (operational) or that they are one-off capital projects. Warren Buffett labels these cyclical and predictable large expenses OpEx, not CapEx. Even though OpEx include predictable day-to-day expenses such as wages, rent, utilities, and insurance, large one-off projects could also be considered OpEx. In either case, working with your financial team and accounting experts to properly categorize these expenses is a sound business practice.

54 According to the Center for Medicare and Medicaid Services, cited in "High Staff Turnover: A Job Quality Crisis in Nursing Homes," The National Consumer Voice for Quality Long-Term Care, September 8, 2022, https://theconsumervoice.org/uploads/files/issues/High_Staff_Turnover-A_Job_Quality_Crisis_in_Nursing_Homes.pdf.

55 The measure of 2,000 hours annually reflects the sum of 40 hours a week for 52 weeks (2,080), minus an average of two weeks for time off.

56 According to the Society for Human Resource Management, cited in "Essential Elements of Employee Retention," Lynchburg Regional SHRM, October 29, 2017, https://lrshrm.shrm.org/blog/2017/10/essential-elements-employee-retention.

57 Intel co-founder Andy Grove preached this in his book *High Output Management* (Vintage, 1995), which is my favorite book on effective management and training practices.

58 I want to make it crystal clear that my point is NOT to go slow and try to anticipate or avoid all risk through group decision-making. Nor am I saying that most decisions should be made based on consensus. I am arguing that briefly slowing down at times to ensure no key conversations are missing, that people are truly aligned and trusting one other, and that you are still headed in the right direction will prevent engine blowups from occurring down the road. These brief conversations are like the oil changes to the organizational engine. Neglect them for too long and all momentum eventually stops.

59 Both Apple and Amazon are famous for eliminating PowerPoint from high-stakes meetings, preferring instead to force team members to hash things out, talk them through, and explain them in their own words. To think together through talk. See Geoffrey James, "The Real Reason Steve

Jobs Hated PowerPoint," *Inc.*, February 5, 2020, https://www.inc.com/geoffrey-james/steve-jobs-hated-powerpoint-you-should-too-heres-what-to-use-instead.html; and Justin Bariso, "Amazon Has a Secret Weapon Known as 'Working Backwards'—and It Will Transform the Way You Work," *Inc.*, December 16, 2019, https://www.inc.com/justin-bariso/amazon-uses-a-secret-process-for-launching-new-ideas-and-it-can-transform-way-you-work.html.

60 This assumes they strategically built a leadership team with diverse and complementary strengths and problem-solving skills instead of a team of clones.

61 The Platinum Rule is leading others how *they* need to be led based on their drives, needs, and behaviors, rather than how *you* want to be led. It is also called "leading to the need" and can be achieved more easily when an organization uses and shares people analytics, data, and reports with all of its team members.

62 Eric Eisenberg's article "Ambiguity as Strategy in Organizational Communication," published in 1984 in *Communication Monographs*, discusses how organizations can strategically use ambiguous messaging as part of a communication strategy. But even with strategically ambiguous messaging, a message is at least being shared and discussed. With missing conversations, there are only gaps and guesses.

63 From Parrish's book, *Clear Thinking* (p. 209).

64 Brian Glazer's book, *A Curious Mind*, is an excellent example of how consciously developing conversational curiosity can payoff big dividends.

65 See https://hbr.org/2024/05/the-art-of-asking-smarter-questions.